P9-CFT-564

TWO FORCES Final 8.5 x 11 f #12

Two forces of opposite extremes are constantly working on us wanting to gain control of our life. Here are some of the facts about these two forces.

[1] They are unseen being spiritual. The things that are seen are temporal and the things that are not seen are eternal. One force guides to eternal life and the other to eternal damnation.
[2] The two forces cause a battle in the mind. Evil forces can sift us as wheat.
[3] One is good or righteous and the other is bad or evil. All good things are of God and all bad things come from Satan but God has the power to have all evil to work together for good.
[4] The good force starts in our spirit. God is a spirit and they that worship Him must worship Him in spirit and truth. The evil starts in the mind and wants preeminence over the good.
[5] Neither the good nor the bad can be proven by man except for the general knowledge that they exist. Most stories on Television and in books are concerning good vs. bad.
[6] If we do not choose the good the evil force takes over.
[7] The force in control can be manifested to ourselves and others. The Bible talks about the manifestations of these two forces in Galatians 5:19-23.
[8] The evil force can take control without our knowledge.
[9] The good force will be by our choice and will be revealed to us by being part of us.
[10] Either one of these two forces can transform us; it will be the one or the other.
[12] These 2 forces have a reflection in everything that happens in the life of each individual.
[13] Every relationship we have with others will be good or bad. Almost every story on television and in books, related to good and bad. Each story to have a pleasant ending the good wins out over the bad. Each individual will have the two forces follow them constantly.
[14] The Bible talks about these two forces over and over again but the bad will win out over the good by an extreme margin; read Matthew 7:21-22.
[15] This whole book will talk about these two forces and the struggles that mankind has regarding them. Many say hell is right here on this earth. Heaven starts on the earth also.
[16] Mental anguish can be a result of the struggle between the two forces. The world has many names to distinguish the bad force as diseases.

PREFACE

All denominations today believe that we are in the apostate age of time. This is where the dispensation of Grace will be terminated. At the present time the Gentile church is disobedient. In the last 60 years the number of evangelical Christian churches has decreased in number to where only about 10 percent of the population of America have spiritual fellowship. Many think that there is no hope for the church unless there is a great revival. I am not too sure whether that that revival will take place among the Gentile church from what we see today. We do know that the Jews will open their eyes spiritually when they are about to be completely destroyed. Their Messiah then will come down to deliver the 144,000 Jews that are left. They will follow the Lamb wherever He goes with all purity. The Great Commission will be taken from the Gentiles and given to the Jewish people and they will evangelize the world. The Book of Revelation talks about the Jewish people being re-commissioned in Revelation 7 and 14. The Jewish nation will evangelize the world probably during the millennium. After that the Devil will be lose again to gather together the Gentiles of many nations to come against the Jew with the largest army that has ever been formed. They will siege the Holy City. Before they attack, God will again fight for his chosen people and destroy all their enemies. Seemingly this is when the world will come to an end and be destroyed by fire.

INTRODUCTION

My book, REMEMBERING MY LIFE, has been well received in my home town of Utica, New York by Christians and non-Christians as well. That includes Protestants of all denominations and Catholics. It is the interpretations of Scriptures that has cause the corruption in religion. The Commands of Jesus are pretty well understood by all. The two most important ones are: The Great Commandment and the Great Commission. The great commandment is to love God and others. The second, the Great Commission, can only be fulfilled by having the first commandment of love. God is love and is above any love this world has to offer. Any man that loves the things of this world have not the love of God. Marriage falls short from God's love except for the fact both the man and the woman must leave their mother and father and become one with each other and God. To do this each marriage partner must agree together what God's Word says which makes them one with Jesus and the Father. John 17:21. The Father and the son must be one with the believer. God's bride includes whosoever will come to Him and not just two people as in marriage. The strong doctrinal differences and preferences will lack oneness in the church. That means you can't have a Martin Luther, John Calvin, John Wesley or Saint Augustine in the same church. History tells us when two the above got together for the first time, they greeted each other with brotherly love. But after hours of talking about doctrine the love left and they didn't see each again in their whole life except for one brief moment. This is what Jesus talks about as doctrine of men. The commandment of love that Jesus gives us takes preeminence to all the other commandments. It you love one another there is no occasion of stumbling. To made known the invisible righteous God would be impossible if one didn't have love that was beyond the understanding of this world Ephesians 3:19. All doctrine and commands of Christ are hinged on the doctrine of love. The love that draw male and female together is similar to the love that attracts man to God. If I be lifted up I will draw all men unto Me. The love that draws man and women together is connected with lust but the love of God is pure genuine love which is given to us by obedience. We learn obedience by suffering. Christ on the cross shows us that way. If we suffer with Him we will also reign with Him.

2

TABLE OF CONTENTS

CHAPTER 1 HABITS MAKE YOU OR BREAK YOU

I do not remember anything when I was a baby but the routine is the same for us all. The routine was two items: eat and sleep. When I was hungry I would cry and when that condition was met I would be content and I would fall to sleep until I got hungry again. A mother's caring for her baby is a lot of hard work that goes on day and night. But because of a mother's love she is happy to do it. As a child grows, the brain begins to function and when his muscles develop he gets up and walks and begins to talk. Parents love it when the child takes his first step and says his first word.

Physical maturity has its problems. If parents do not teach spiritual maturity at the same time, the child's physical maturity will leave behind the Godlike image in which He created us all.

From that time the child starts to form habits. Parents form the baby's habits of eating and sleeping. At that time, spiritual habits should be developed to help your child form righteous conversations and acts before the child is capable of talking or doing anything. This is done by introducing their child to a righteous God.

Parents should start reading the Bible to their children even before they understand. The first Bible verse that I understood as a newborn babe in Christ is found in *Ephesians 5:17* "be not unwise but understanding what the will of the Lord is." That verse stayed with me all my life because of the need, and there is still the need for it.

As a child increases his mental and physical abilities, habits will be formed. As a baby, he or she cries when they are hungry. This is logical, but that logic will continue as growth sets in. The child will now want what he sees and will cry out until he gets what he wants. This nature will continue to form habits. By the act of the mother feeding her baby, she actually helps the child form the first habit; eating is a habit and can turn into a bad habit later in life by eating too much or the wrong food. The mother and father should form new habits in their children by first demonstrating them in their own lives. Having a child believe in an unseen righteous God is easy. To have them form Godly habits will be the challenge. It depends on how the parents talk and act in daily life. Children are created in the image of God. It is in their spirit to understand God, but when bad habits are allowed to be formed it allows sin to enter. You do not have to teach a child a bad habit. It is part of their inbred nature. Parents must teach their children good habits to be part of their new nature.

Many children grow up with bad habits because the flesh is stronger than the spirit. So raising a child up in forming good habits should continue as a daily procedure.

Proverbs 22:6 "Train up a child in the way he should go: and when he is old, he will not depart from it." This verse means that habits can be lasting. But it is so easy to let bad habits creep in.

Even if you do train a child the right way, peer pressures come when a child grows up and he will have strong temptations. There comes a time when every child will be on his own in this world, so he must discipline himself to follow the righteousness of the Lord Jesus Christ. The love that the child is taught in the home can be contaminated by peer pressure as the child goes out into this world.

The question is: since all grownups have formed some bad habits, how are they changed? This is the cry of every teenager, "How can I break a bad habit?"

I only see one way. That one way is based on *Second Corinthians 5:17* "Therefore if any man be in Christ, he is a new creature: old things are passed away; behold, all things are become new." What this verse is simply saying is that the new habit must have the old habit pass away.

First of all, everyone knows that to form a good habit takes time. Many say a habit must be repeated daily for a period of time before it is formed. Many scholars say that it is daily from 30 to 40 days.

We can't understand how much we need good habits until we see how wrong the bad habits are. This is why sin gets deeper and deeper until a person will come and recognize his sin and has a determination to come out of his sin. When that happens, the old habit will help remind us of the new habit we want to form.

If a person robs you of your wallet it is easy to become angry. That actually permits the sin of the robber to make you sin. We can't see it that way because we are focused on the wrong that the other person did to us. Your justification will have you focus on the other person and not yourself. That is why it is easier to see the sin of others much more rapidly than you can see your own sin. This is called judging. The Bible says that we are judging when we see the wrong of others but do not see sin in our own life.

Matthew 7:1-5 The last verse says to first confess your sin so you can clearly see how to help the other person to see his sin. Even if he has robbed you, your sin is greater than his sin. In your anger you may even desire to take vengeance. This is how sin is handed down from generation to generation. We may want to do the right thing but the sin of others will lead us into sin.

The first step in forming a good habit is to see your bad habits as sin. The devil will help you do that. In fact he will torment you continually with the thought of the other person who sinned against you. But that is actually the way God can help you. Each time the devil torments you, it's necessary to superimpose that negative character quality to a positive character quality of Christ. The fruits of the spirit are character qualities, so you choose one that goes against what character quality Satan gave you. In this case you need to cast out anger and superimpose it with love. Now you say, how can I be angry with the person I love? It is the people you know the best that can irritate you the most. *Second Corinthians 10:5* "Casting down

imaginations, and every high thing that exalteth itself against the knowledge of God, and bringing into captivity every thought to the obedience of Christ..."

That is going to make you feel like a hypocrite because your feelings are stronger than the truth. But what are you going to believe, the truth or your reasoning? The first time you do this, do not expect your feelings to be conquered. Feelings are the last thing to change after falling into temptation. You must build your new habit on faith which is God's Word. So every time the torment comes, superimpose it with love. It may be a hundred times the first day. Remember the first day doesn't create a habit. You may have to do it for forty days. The paradox is that it may take a long time to form the new habit, but when it is formed, it will be all of a sudden. You can be thinking of the person who robbed your wallet and all of a sudden you love him. Now, that is a miracle and you will know that God did it. This is how we get to know the love of God. It is above romance. Do not think getting married will be the greatest thing that happened to you. It is so easy to replace God's love with human love. Marriage was created by God to show us love but human love can fail. If you get divorced it may be the worst thing that has ever happened to you. Considering that many couples are only living together now instead of getting married, the divorce rate is now 87 percent and not the 50 percent that we have been hearing for the last twenty years.

CHAPTER 2 GENUINE LOVE

Lack of genuine love will do two things, and those things are destroying the church today. First, the lack of love is when others do us wrong. This has caused more divisions than anything else. Second, a lack of love will keep us from winning the lost and bringing them to Christ. We are not all called to be an apostle but we are to be a disciple in the environment where we live, which includes our family, friends, colleagues, workmates, and people we meet in the course of a day. If they do not see and hear Jesus coming from you, you may be influencing them the wrong way.

When we show love, people will want to talk to us. It is only then that we can minister the Gospel. I have a joy in witnessing to people but it didn't happen overnight. For years I obeyed the command to witness without feeling the joy. That only restricted me from the joy that could be had.

It is so easy to react toward others. This reaction is the major reason why there is no joy in the Christian life. We can't have joy when we react. Reaction to the wrongs others do to you will always create negative character qualities.

God loved the world so much that He gave His Son. If we follow that example the Bible says there will be no occasion of stumbling in us. What that means is to love people who offend us.

Human nature causes us to react against them, which is exchanging evil for evil. I have to believe what God said is true. It is quite simple: if I confess my sins every time I get upset, I am forgiven. It becomes a learning process, so I can learn to love even my enemy. Learning to love your enemy starts with loving the ones who you know the best. If I don't love the people whom I live with, how can I expect to love my enemies?

I have stayed in many homes in my travels around the world. Parents love their children but they have a hard time showing it when their children are disobedient. Parents tend to argue back when their children rebel. I saw this so much but I didn't have any answers at the time. This is where so many Christian parents lose their children. (The parents can't see their own sin.) The first step to love your enemy is to confess your lack of love. When I was offended I realized it was easy to see the other person's sin but not my own sin. (I didn't see that I had sinned when the other person was wrong.) I never realized it but the first step was for me to confess my own sin in order for me to help the offender with his sin. (When a person's focus is on the sin of others, he can't see himself for what he is.) The other person can be more wrong than us and that doesn't matter. All it does is make us feel more justified.

CHAPTER 3 A LOVING HOME

Four things parents need to learn and they all concern love:
1. They should not get angry when Disciplining.
2. They should confess when they are wrong.
3. They should be faithful to do what they say they will do.
4. They should praise their children when they are obedient.

The sad thing to see is a child having a wrong relationship with their parents. The parents are not right when they correct their children in anger and the children are in no position to tell their parent when they are angry. When this happens, love starts to disintegrate.

Devotional time is meeting with a loving God. The family can prove this by loving one another. During devotions the children must be given the right to tell the parent when they are wrong but they must have a clear conscience. God proved His love by taking our wrong (sin) when He was right (having no sin). When the family argues, each member who argues is trying to prove that the other is wrong. Jesus tells us to love our enemies. That would be a good family discussion, to find out how to love family members before they become enemies.

Being in full agreement is so much needed. People have asked me: "How can we agree with somebody we know is wrong?" The problem is, when I think someone else is wrong, I presume that I am right. If I think I am right, I need patience to give God time to change the other person, but being upset and complaining does not do it. The culprit is the person who has a negative attitude. Hate, anger, bitterness, envy is all work of the devil. Many times both sides have wrong attitudes.

If only two Christians would agree together, God would answer their request. *Matthew 18:18-20.* But first, any past disagreement must be cleared up. *Matthew 5: 23-28.* Even Daniel had to confess his own sins in order to help others with their sins. *Daniel 9:20.*

This means I have to love people who disagree with me. You may not see disagreement as sin, yet almost every church has had splits that started over a disagreement, and marriages have the same problem. I believe Christians must be disciplined in love. A child is rich in faith but he or she must learn to grow in Love. *First Corinthians 13*, the love chapter, says, "When I was a Child I spoke as a child, I thought as a child, I understood as a child but when I became a man I put away childish things." A child lives on the love of his parents to provide for him but a child can't distinguish between wants and needs. Adults are no better when they want money and things, thinking it is the way God will bless them.

I went to churches that believed that God blesses us by giving us riches. Maybe others did not believe this in doctrine but people do brag about how God blessed them when they receive materialistic pleasures. I thought that so deeply and for so long that it just became part of my thinking. It is wrong thinking; God wants to bless us when we obey Him. "It is more blessed to give than to receive." *Acts 20:35* "If you love me, keep my commandments." *John 14:15*

Parents spoil their children by giving them the things of the world instead of the things of God. But, many times, parents lose out in the same way, by having too many playthings. When Jesus started His ministry He had no home, no spending money, and no rights. *Philippians 2:5-8*

I haven't been to Ecuador now for five years but I receive phone calls from a family about every six months. I lived with them for a while and introduced them to a family Bible time. It was an enjoyment that I'll never forget

either. This made us love one another with a godly love.

CHAPTER 4 THE KEY IS LOVE

My biggest lack at one time was understanding why God sent Jesus to this world. It was because God so *loved* the world. Christ ascended into heaven so we can have this *love* to continue to do what Jesus started by the Holy Spirit. *1 John 4:19* "We love Him because He first loved us."

After some Scripture searching I believe I have found the answer. I should have known that the answer would be in loving others because that was my problem and it is the greatest of all Christ's commandments. It is called the Great Commandment: To *love* God and others with all your heart, mind, soul, and strength. We have a need for love in order to be happy. God made us that way. Marriage is to give us some understanding of love, but marriage comes short of God's pure love. God's love is genuine for everyone, not just two people in marriage. A person can be satisfied with God's love without getting married. Marriage is just a small portion of God's love for us. I have seen such a lack of love while staying in homes when I was traveling. I thought to myself, "If I got married I probably would have the same problem." Young couples are so in love that they think they will live happily ever after and with a few marriages that does happen.

Genuine love is a marriage with Jesus and it is not limited to a marriage of two people. Sex is not love. In the Old Testament each time a person had sex he had to purify himself. See Lev. chapters 14-15.

There will be no marriages in Heaven because romance is not a qualifying factor. In marriage, romance is necessary. When romance leaves, the marriage grows cold.

One of my greatest desires was to get married. But I saw marriage as a personal desire. The problem with personal desire is that God's love can be pushed aside. Many young people when dating do not make room for God, they are having too much fun in romance. That was my problem. I was having too much fun living in the world. In most homes where I have stayed as a traveling missionary, family time with the Bible and prayer seems very religious. Is it any wonder children do not look forward to family devotions? They can't have any fun with God. God is reverent but also love, joy, and peace.

After years of observing family life in the homes I had visited, I see why marriages have problems. There is more of a religious atmosphere than one of serving a righteous God. Religion is reading the Bible and praying together. Practicing righteousness is acquiring the character qualities of Jesus, to be more like Jesus. That is fun!

Young people have so much love for the opposite sex that when a Christian meets a nonbeliever they think that after marriage, the partner will accept the Lord, but that rarely happens.

Subconsciously we humans place marriage as our ultimate love because it is so emotional. Romance and sex is what makes it so emotional. That is why marriage is only between two people and God has many restrictions to keep it that way. God's love is to bring everyone together in oneness. See John 17:23.

David said that Jonathan's love for him was greater than the love for woman. That is God's love, which is not an attraction in the flesh but in the spirit which everyone has. God is a Spirit and has given each of us a spirit to have a joyful relationship together. It starts with our spirit communing with our mind, then to our will, and last of all to our feelings. In that order. Feeling is the last of the transactions. Last but not least. When I feel that I love God everything else has a worthless meaning. The flesh is the other way around. "The spirit is willing but the flesh is weak." The flesh has feelings that are motivated with lust. Then we hear a voice, "That feels good let us do it again." The feelings come first and many times these

feelings will overcome the mind, the will, and the spirit. This is why self-discipline is so important.

Love, joy, and peace are the fruit of the spirit. If we involve our five senses with love, joy and peace it can be of the world which involves lust and the Scriptures say "love not the world nor the things of the world." *1 John 2:15* We can have fun but when Satan is in control it will lead into sin. It is our five senses that Satan uses to entangle us into lust and all that is of the World is lust. See 1 John 2:16.

When married people realize they need to live in forgiveness for each other they will find that it isn't romance that is the binding factor in intimacy. Intimacy is a word usually given to one's sex life but the word is wrongly used if it doesn't bring oneness and unity in good and bad things.

First Corinthian 13 shows that the aspects of God's love in romance are not mentioned. In fact there is something in that chapter that I did not understand for a long time: *First Corinthians 13:12* "... Now we know in part but then shall we be known fully just as I also have been fully known." I used to think that kind of love was only found in heaven, but the Scriptures in context indicate we can understand God's genuine love right here on earth. Love is needed so our relationship with Jesus can be perfected to reach people for Christ. That is what real marriage is all about. It is to unite all people together in Christ and without lust.

CHAPTER 5 LOVE IN THE CHURCH

When I accepted the Lord the church never showed me love in discipleship. Maturity came with time. If I was a Christian for a long period of time, I was thought to be more mature. What a false concept that is. For this reason I was never able to disciple others. Many leaders think if someone wants to go into ministry they need to leave the church and go to Bible school, or college and seminary. Knowledge of the Bible doesn't give a person virtue and character. I should have been taught this by a mature Christian in the church. I had to learn to have godly character by the hard knocks of life in traveling to forty-five countries and fifty times through America. If I had a mature Christian with me I would have matured in a few months instead of it taking me years to achieve.

The American church has lost the art of discipleship and accountability because there is no application involving love. Love started with God sacrificing his own begotten Son. And Jesus had to apply this by learning obedience through the things He suffered. That was meant to be an example for His twelve disciples to do the same and to be carried down from generation to generation.

A leader's job is to see that family members have personal devotions and family devotions on a daily basis. After that they need to understand what application is and the difference between doctrine and application. God will give each of us an application at least once a day for the rest of our lives. Doctrine will be the same for the whole church but application will be different. We will be in trouble if we make application our doctrine. There should be one doctrine for all of God's people and many applications to give us daily guidance. Today we have many different doctrines and we forget about application.

Application is done by personally using the Bible in finding out why God allows daily difficulties in life. We need to learn obedience through daily struggles by counting tribulation as joy. See James 1:2. Jesus had to learn obedience by the things that He suffered to set an example for me. This is the main reason for meditation on the Scriptures. I can spend a couple of hours in meditation before I find an application concerning a decision that needs to be made or how to relate to a conflict or some situation that I face. God allows many things to happen daily and when we meditate on Scripture He will guide us. All we need to do is to find time for God in His Word.

It is unbelievable how many times God wanted to give me Grace to overcome my reactions and make me part of His church. I was made to believe that a church is just a building. The best that people can do in a church building is to learn knowledge. The sad thing is that the Scriptures do not change a person until there is a demonstration in everyday life. Jesus started the process by daily demonstrating to his disciples in public. When I didn't receive God's grace in my life, my sufferings were in vain. We should do what is right and suffer for it. That is found by self-control not by knowledge. *First Peter 2:19-25* "If you do well and suffer for it this is acceptable with God." *Hebrews 12:1-5* "[1]Wherefore seeing we also are compassed about with so great a cloud of witnesses, let us lay aside every weight, and the sin which doth so easily beset us, and let us run with patience the race that is set before us, [2] Looking unto Jesus the author and finisher of our faith; who for the joy that was set before him endured the cross, despising the shame, and is set down at the right hand of the throne of God. [3] For consider him that endured such, contradiction of sinners against himself, lest you be wearied and faint in your minds.[4] You have not yet resisted unto blood, striving against sin. [5]And you have forgotten exhortation which speaks unto you as unto children, my son, despise not thou the chastening of the Lord, nor faint when thou art rebuked of him..."

There are a number of Scriptures telling us how to get joy. Notice, underlined below, that joy can come through suffering. Jesus set the example by living on the basic essentials and then dying for us when He did nothing wrong. Jesus died because of the joy set before Him, referring to his suffering. We also would have joy if we are willing to suffer without complaining.

James 1:2-3 [2]My brethren, count it all joy when you fall into divers temptations;

[3]Knowing this, that the trying of your faith works patience.

Matthew 5:11-12 [11]Blessed are ye, when men shall revile you, and persecute you, and shall say all manner of evil against you falsely, for my sake. [12]Rejoice, and be exceeding glad: for great is your reward in heaven: for so persecuted they the prophets which were before you.

It is not necessary to suffer for the sins that we are willing to put on the cross. When we suffer for our own sin, it is putting Christ on the cross and not allowing Christ to die for our sins. Judas had to suffer for his own sin. It is called the sin unto death or the unpardonable sin. Every time we have a wrong attitude, we are headed in the wrong direction. Every time I argued while talking to sinners or Christians I was heading in the wrong direction. If we do that long enough, it can be a river of no return.

The church's role is to train leaders. When I was in the US Army I had training by leaders who were trained by others. Preaching is such a small part of training and yet over 90 percent of the church is preaching.

CHAPTER 6 MY LACK OF LOVE

As I re-read my life story I notice a trend that was not good. When I disagreed with someone I would always get into conflict. With my commitment to travel from New York to California I had something to brag about when I left all my possessions behind. I left them behind me but they were still inside of me. Since people looked up to me because of that commitment I kept bragging about it, for I had nothing else to prove that I was a Christian except some good works. That was until I received discipleship with Christians in Action where I understood that Christianity was a life of obedience to God's Word.

When I received discipleship I wondered why I had to struggle with three things: wanting riches, immoral thoughts, and pride. I tried so hard to cleanse myself of

these three things and I would make progress but slip right back to wrong thinking. This process continued for years. Then the Lord showed me that my failure was because of bad habits that were not conquered after I became a Christian. When I started to confess my sins, it was a step in the right direction.

My biggest problem was not living in harmony with other Christians. It was not my nature to love when in disagreement. This has happened with every organization I have worked with. When I got off on my own, the suffering increased because I wanted to do what I thought was right in my own eyes. If we suffer with Christ we will reign with Him. Suffering for doing what is right only comes by loving your enemy. Many times our enemy is in our own camp. The Jewish people had the law but there was no application to the law in their own life. They ended up forcing the law on others but with no love. That is like forcing your children to obey without love. It just doesn't work. It causes reaction.

Nevertheless, learning to confess my own sins was seriously needed if I was going to help the church. No doubt the church is living in apostasy today. Every leader knows that we are living in the era of apostasy but they can't put their finger on what to do about it. I believe even the best of churches are leading toward apostasy. That is mainly because the church is not having new converts. Love for the lost is missing. And if love is missing for the lost it is also missing for the ones you live with. Jesus loves us all equally. He even loved Judas unto the end.

CHAPTER 7 A LOVE FOR PEOPLE

Some time ago I made a commitment to witnessing to everyone I talked to. That was the greatest bondage that I ever had but it was only for two weeks. It was one of the greatest commitments I made because now I witness to almost everyone I talk to without the bondage. I still need to pray for love because I never know when Satan will turn

11

someone against me. It has happened a few times and when it happens it will be unexpected. The person will become so radical that you would think I killed their daughter. I'll say I'm sorry but nothing seems to help. It is like the person wants to kill Jesus and me also. Usually I'll say nothing more and leave.

Jesus took his twelve disciples everywhere with him to set an example of public ministry. When Jesus was arrested, He told his persecutors, "I spoke openly and I kept nothing secret. Ask the people that heard me." *John 18:20-21*. All through the Gospels the word "preach" is only used in reference to public speaking. When Jesus spoke in the synagogues the Scriptures used the word "teach."

This is what is lacking today, the church needs to witness in public daily. Preaching in the church rarely does much good. The sermon is forgotten when the service is over. Very few takes notes. When I was in Ecuador there was a saying that if the Missionary doesn't apply his sermon to himself it would be completely wasted.

This morning I stopped at a post office and noticed that the clerk was training a new worker. I mentioned that I like to train people to enter into a new life so they can go to heaven. They both agreed that was a good idea. I said that many church people are religious but they have no idea how to be righteous. That got their attention. I continued to explain that unrighteousness is disagreeing and having a conflict over what each thinks is right, and then nobody wins.

Righteousness is just the opposite. A child of God needs to love people who disagree with him. That means to love your enemy, bless them who curse you, do good to them who hate you and pray for them who persecute you. That got their full attention so I continued for about ten minutes. I know that made an impact on them because I was blessed. It filled me with joy for the whole day.

When others receive the Gospel we become one in Christ. This is really the only

thing worth living for. When Christians agree with you about Scripture we become one in Christ, and if any two people will agree on any one thing it will be done for them likewise. The problem in the world is that when we disagree with someone we want to immediately speak what we think is right. See 1 Corinthians. 6:16-17.

As Jesus took His disciples publicly, He witnessed to the multitudes that followed Him. Witnessing publicly was how Jesus trained His disciples.

Our only public appearance today is mixing with others in association with the love of worldly attractions and having conversations about everything but our Creator. On television, there is not a program that doesn't promote superstars for their intelligence and abilities mixed with lust and profane language. If I can't discipline myself when I am alone, I do not stand a chance in the presence of other undisciplined people, including Christians.

CHAPTER 8 THE SECRET OF DISCIPLESHIP

The secret of discipleship is love. Jesus loved Judas until the end. It was not Jesus that brought Judas's life to an end. Judas grieved the Holy Spirit by rejecting the love of God and had nothing to live for. The end of Judas came by his own action of committing suicide.

Love is the most powerful way to be like Jesus. God's love is so necessary to love your enemies and to have your love rise up above lust. All love pertaining to this world the Bible says is lust. Everything is lust for what you feel or lust for what you want. That is called the lust of the flesh or the lust of the eyes. Young Christians dating each other have a hard time having joy in talking about the Bible. Their attraction for each other will rise up above their attraction for God. We can only change from lust to genuine love by what we think. Think of Jesus as though He is our bridegroom, and He has more than one bride. All the brides together are called the church of Christ. You can't lust and have Jesus at the same time.

David made a statement that Jonathan's love for him was wonderful, passing the love of women. 1 Samuel 18:1. The Scriptures also say that ". . . Jonathan loved David with his own soul." *2 Samuel 1:26.* Jesus said that we need to love God with our whole heart. And with all our soul, with all our mind. Matt. 22:37-38. Mark includes: with all your understanding and with all your strength. Mark 12:33. Also in Luke 10:27. If we put that all together I think we all need to reexamine our love for God. It is much more than I thought it could be. Every time I talk about Jesus my love helps me overcome wicked people and lust.

Love convicts others when they are wrong or love will cause others to be jealous and persecute you. Telling others about Jesus brings out the true heart of a person. "How a man thinks in his heart, so is he." God will give us this love to draw others to Christ. When we are pleasing to the Lord we have a transfer of love and when we use that love to reach people, our Father's love will be confirmed in us. Is it that hard to understand? Obedience brings blessings and disobedience brings cursing. Deuteronomy Chapter 28 has a whole chapter to show what happens when there is obedience and disobedience. It shouldn't be any wonder that we learn obedience by the things we suffer. We suffer for the bad we do, or we suffer for the good we do. We suffer for our own sins or let Jesus suffer for our sins. Either way it is suffering. It is hard to think that Jesus would want to suffer for our sins. Human nature wants to destroy others who come against us. Suffering and blessings will follow us all through life. If we suffer the right way, we will be blessed without the Lust. If one suffers the wrong way he will curse God. Isn't it common that whenever something bad happens people will take Christ's name in vain, and even louder than someone praising God? Saying the name of Jesus can be a blessing, but when evil happens people will use His name as a curse without thinking about it.

Discipline in the church must also be done in love. Almost always, when another Christian is in sin they will react against you. They will never confess that they are wrong and many times it will result in a church division. It may be one person or half the church. A good leader will never react back to the one in sin. Love needs to go into action. Because Jesus loved Judas there was no conflict. Judas even confessed that he betrayed innocent blood before he killed himself. So close to repentance, but Judas only went halfway. God wants our whole heart or none at all.

CHAPTER 9 BURNOUT

We have a hard time overcoming stress by ourselves. We need the comfort of others. But isn't that another name of the Holy Spirit: "The Comforter"? The Scriptures tell us that we can have the mind of Christ and the comfort of the Holy Spirit.

2 Timothy 1:7 When God blesses us it is not with the things of the world. In fact, in Acts 20:35 for physical things it is more blessed to give than to receive. *1 John 2:15* says, anyone who has the love of the world, the love of God is not in him.

The greatest blessing a man can have is to have all temptation taken away. God can't have fellowship with Satan so when God is in you to do His will, all temptation has to leave. I call this a visitation of the Holy Spirit. As long as a Christian hangs on to anger or bitterness he will not be able to have the spirit of God in him. But if you confess your anger God will cleanse you from all unrighteousness. It will be like that in heaven always. What is loosed in heaven will be loosed on earth also, but not continuously. I have had visitations from the Holy Spirit for as long as three days straight. I usually will get a visitation at least once a week. We all have this hope, but we have earthly feelings from divine intervention, which is a feeling of true happiness. These visitations appeared to Paul when he was in great stress. The greater the temptation the greater the blessing. It is hard to imagine the conflict Paul went through but there were blessings that went along with that. Good and bad will follow us wherever we go. The bad isn't falling into temptation but enduring the temptation. He that endures until the end the same shall be saved. Satan's counterpart in the flesh is to deceive us. This morning I thought of a person who had tormented me. Others agree that he has an evil spirit, but that wasn't enough to comfort me. My morning devotions told me my part. *1 John 3:14* ". . . he that loves not his brother abides in death."

Right after I was saved I heard stories of pastors having nervous breakdowns. That confused me. When I asked why, the response was something that wasn't confirmed to be right within my spirit. They would say, "Stress sometimes overcomes us." Almost every Christian knows *2 Timothy 1:7*: "God has not given us the spirit of fear, but of power, love and of a sound mind."

As a missionary I have approached burnout over and over again. But each time it was because of sin that brought me into conflict. Each time I am in conflict I have depression. Now I see the danger of conflict in my own soul. I have made it a habit to confess my sin to God and others every time I approach burnout. The problem is that sometimes I wait too long before confessing it. Burnout is nothing more than thinking on the negative, which is where Satan takes control. I'm not saying that all depression is because of conflict. Many illnesses can cause depression also.

Changing our attitudes toward people helps us to stay positive. We control people more than we think. Isn't it obvious when you show love to a person he will express love back to you? But if you are angry with a person, he will react likewise to you. We make others good or bad by our own positive or negative gestures. It is the way sin is handed down from generation to generation.

Live like Jesus is in us. The second Adam, being Jesus, handed down righteousness. That is why the promise of salvation is for you and your children. Righteousness is handed down by Jesus versus Sin being handed down by Adam and Eve. The best of us have had the devil deceive us at times, but God gives others the ability to see the sin in our life before we do. Our emotions can hide our sin, but others that know us who are emotionally free of the situation can see our sin clearly. This is why we need accountability. When we cannot help ourselves we need others to help us. We need to be careful because Satan would have us judge rather than to help. Judging is seeing the sin of the other person without having love for him. With humility we can let others help us. But with pride, we will react badly and destroy our self along with others. Everything in the Christian life depends on our attitude. "Let this mind be in you which was also in Christ Jesus." *Phil. 2:5*

CHAPTER 10 GOD VERSUS SATAN

God has positive ways to control people and Satan also has negative ways to control people. Satan comes to steal, kill, and destroy and it is all done by deceiving us with his temptations and his efforts to appear as an angel of light to destroy us. Righteousness and evil mixed together is all darkness. It is very easy to deceive people with half-truths. Satan will be destroyed and he wants to take as many as he can with him. We need to love each other and that includes loving our enemies.

I found out that if I can't love my enemies, I can't love my friends. If I am angry with one person it ruins my whole day. The Bible says if we love our brother there is no occasion of falling. This is where Satan has a hold today. Almost every church has a lack of brotherly love, which causes conflicts and divisions in the church, yet in the church during the service there is praise and worship. Our praise and worship should also be with each other outside the four walls of the church. How often do we praise our own family in their presence? How we act toward others is what we are toward God. Jesus says, "What you have done to the least of these you have done to me." Many conflicts come by not keeping our promises. That seems like a little thing but it can turn people against each other.

The procedure is simple. Daily we find people coming against us in anger, disagreement, or just with a negative disposition. If any of those attributes come to your mind when you make contact with the person, you might as well surrender any possibility of having love toward the person. The simple solution is to confess your negative attitude. Breathe a word of prayer: "I'm sorry Lord for that wrong thought and I want the love of Jesus for them." Many times we all know this, so why do we fall into the trap over and over again. Love always takes at least two people. Find someone you can have accountability with to remind you of this. Husbands and wives should do this all the time. When they practice this love and acceptance on others it will also help in their relationship with each other.

In the home today there is a divorce rate of over 87 percent, not 50 percent as we hear most of the time. In fact, I have heard it was 50 percent for the last fifty years. Fornication and adultery are everyday practices now, no longer is it against civil law. Fifty years ago adultery was against the law and so was divorce and remarriage. Now we are more law abiding than God abiding. This is the way Satan works. His power is in the tree of Good and Evil. That means we can be like God by knowing what is right and wrong. If we fall for that lie, it means we don't need Jesus as our savior. To know what is right and wrong in everything, we would not need the knowledge of God. We must discern evil, not learn what is evil. Learning evil is not positive thinking. Love is always thinking of godly attributes. Memorize the fruit of the spirit. When I think on anything negative I

might as well forget telling others about Jesus. Others may not know you have a negative spirit but God does and He doesn't like hypocrites. You can't speak of love and have negative thoughts.

Satan tempts people we come in fellowship with to think just the opposite of what we think. What some think is good, the other will think is wrong. This is how Satan gets us to disagree and come into an argument. (See Chapter 4, Jim Dixon in my life story: REMEMBERING MY LIFE...)

Love in marriage is an act of God. It is God that attracts the opposite sex, not lust. Lust is the devil's temptation. The mind must be trained with self-discipline. God gives men and women this love on a silver platter. This love is called "first love." As time passes the husband and wife see things differently. Men and women have different ways of thinking and that will bring them into disagreements. So the "first love" given by God can only continue by our not reacting when in a disagreement. Pure love is not based on what people like to do together. If you love them that love you what reward have you? The reward comes when you live in forgiveness. See the story of Lowell Barrett in Chapter 4 IN MY LIFE STORY. (Is there irony in life?).

Years ago when computers first came out, Art Linkletter teamed up young couples by the things that they had in common interest. Out of 50,000 young men and women who were teamed up only four of them got married and three of them ended up divorced. He then realized that it is un-likes that attract. That is why marriages must always live in forgiveness. Love is the first fruit of the spirit and temperance is the last. Love is impossible without self-discipline. All nine items in the fruit of the spirit must work together as one.

We are living in God's grace through Jesus Christ our Lord. We do not get God's grace for nothing even though it is free. In every promise and command there are preparations for us to act on. To have God's grace there are tests.

CHAPTER 11 GOOD AND BAD

One morning while living in St. Louis, Missouri, I had an accident on the way to work. It was during that time when I realized that good and bad would follow me all through life.

Good and bad will follow us all through life, just like a railroad track. One track being good and one being bad. We need both rails working together where they reinforce one another and only God can do that. Usually, we try to get rid of the bad and keep the good. Grace is the transition between the bad and the good. If you do not take the bad with the right attitude, the good will not be the motivating factor in your life. We all want good, but good is a far cry from righteousness. Man's righteousness is as filthy rags with God. All good things are from God but the good we think is from God can easily be of the world with its lust, riches, and pride. The love, joy, and peace of the fruit of the Spirit can be replaced with a false love, joy, and peace of the world.

1 John 2:15 "Love not the world, neither the things that are in the world. If any man love the world, the love of the Father is not in him." Trying to avoid the bad and cling to the good will destroy us so easily. Resisting the devil and resisting evil are two different things. We should resist the devil but not evil people, or we will not be able to love our enemy. If we do not resist temptation Satan will gain control. If we resist evil people we will not be able to love them. For this reason the Lord gives us an ability to love people and hate their sin. This is the grace of God. If we do not separate the good and evil in people we will react poorly to the evil they do to us. *Matthew 5:39* "But I say unto you, that you resist not evil: but whosoever shall smite thee on thy right cheek, turn to him the other also."

1 Peter 5:8-9 "⁸ Be sober, be vigilant; because your adversary the devil, as a roaring lion, walks about, seeking whom he may devour: ⁹ Whom resist steadfast in the faith, knowing that the same afflictions are accomplished in your brethren that are in the world."

James 4:11-12 "¹¹ Speak not evil one of another, brethren. He that speaketh evil of his brother, and judgeth his brother, speaketh evil of the law, and judgeth the law: but if thou judge the law, thou art not a doer of the law, but a judge. ¹² There is one lawgiver, who is able to save and to destroy: who art thou that judgest another?" We are judging when we put together the sin along with the person who commits the sin. Our government is much like the Old Testament law. "Thou shalt love thy neighbor and hate your enemy; but Jesus says to love your enemy." *Matthew 5:43-44*

In the New Testament God has a way of making Satan's temptations to be beneficial. This is by grace. Grace is given to us to turn the bad into good. We fail the test every time we complain or have negative attitudes.

God makes no distinction between people. God lets the sun rise on the good and the bad and He sends rain on the just and the unjust.

In self-examination I realized that I had good and bad traveling with me all my life. If I strive to get rid of the bad and cling to the good, the good and bad would not serve the purpose they were made for. I did not experience the good and bad at the same time in my life but they were close in time so I would understand the connection. The important thing is to have a positive attitude when the bad comes or you will be resisting God. This is why praising God in all things is so important. It will help us to trust God even in the worse situations.

Some years ago I found out that "praise" is in the Bible 2,000 times. That gave me the understanding that praise was the most important doctrine in the Bible. It seems like man only made Doctrine from Scriptures that is not clear and so the intelligence of man goes into action. The simple things that are easy to understand we have no stress of making doctrine out of it.

One day I wanted to see how many times I could praise God during one day. I found a pen and pad to carry around with me so I could write down all the times I praised God. At the end of the day as I was counting the number of times I praised Him, I stopped dead in my tracks. Counting the number of times was my principle objective until I recognized that I praised God mostly when bad things happened—not when the good happened. It turned out that I only praised God once when I was happy.

I then figured out why. The good gave me too much satisfaction in life to even think about God. The bad showed me that I needed God. But if I was in a fox hole with bullets flying over my head, my prayers would be without ceasing.

The story of Jacob wrestling with the angel is a lesson concerning good and bad. Jacob wanted the blessing and he got it. Blessing here means a transfer of power. The angel transferred his power to Jacob. We can't believe that Jacob was stronger than that angel when Jacob said, "I will not let you go until you bless me." I believe that wrestling match was fixed. God had that match planned before it happened. Jacob got the blessing, but he also got what he didn't want. He went limping away. This experience changed Jacob's life. His name changed from Jacob, meaning a deceiver, to Israel, meaning Prince of God. From this story we learn that good and bad do work together. My lesson is that I need to stop complaining.

One thing I had to watch out for during my adult life was my own lust and pride, both of which could get me into trouble. The good times would come—those were the times I had to watch out for Pride. *2 Corinthians 12:7* "And lest I should be exalted above measure through the abundance of the revelations, there was given to me a thorn in the flesh, the messenger of Satan to buffet me lest I should be exalted above measure."

When the bad times happened, I would complain and get upset. Or I would use lustful thoughts to give me some comfort. It is all sin. Bad times lead us into temptation of complaining. Good times lead us into the sin of pride. Satan has got us coming or going.

If a man only has desires for the good things of life, pride will easily conquer him. We must give thanks in all things. The more one wants to be used for God, it seems like the more one must be willing to suffer with the right attitude, which is to suffer with Christ on the cross. Suffering with a bad attitude is suffering for our own sin but the good side of this is that there are no atheists in a foxhole. It is normal to think of God when in trouble.

Good and bad are found all through life on this earth. All wars are based on what is good and what is bad. In most cases both sides claim to be the good guys. In our country's first war, both the colonies and England claimed they were right. Each war we had after that, we claim to be right. Ever since I was a child, I have loved movies of cowboys and Indians; again both sides claim to be the good guys. Couples sometimes break apart when both husband and wife think they are right. I have traveled through the country over fifty times and I haven't yet seen a church that didn't have a division. Again both sides claim to be right. I believe this is the major reason why the church is decreasing in numbers rapidly. Today most homicides are family related. This sin is passed down to their offspring also.

CHAPTER 12 GOD'S GRACE

I had to learn God's grace through suffering. A Christian will suffer in the way that Jesus suffered but God gives grace to cover this so we can love those who persecute us. That is why we are saved by grace. Because we are sinners, we can learn obedience by the things we suffer. Jesus suffered for doing what is right. We know five things about grace:
1. It is given to all. *Titus 2:11* Grace has appeared to all men.

2. By grace we have salvation. *Ephesians 2:8-9 "By grace are we saved."*
3. We respond to grace, then more is given. *2 Peter 3:18* "Grow in grace."
4. It can be resisted. *James 4:6* "God resists the proud."
5. We must be humble to receive it. *James 4:6* "God gives grace to the humble."

First, grace appears to all men the same way. Pain wants us to resist the bad. We are to resist the devil but not resist evil people (as explained in Chapter 24). God will not have Satan to destroy us but it is a test for us. Temptation is designed to bring disobedience to God, like Satan tempted Adam and Eve to be disobedient. If we reject the bad we are resisting God's grace. Without Christ how can a person stop himself from rejecting the bad? Even as a Christian we need to trust God by praising Him when the bad comes. *Proverbs 3:5-7*

God will not allow us to take more temptation than we can handle. And all things will work together for good to them who love God and are called according to His purpose. The stronger the temptation, the more we can grow in Christ.

CHAPTER 13 TEMPTATIONS AND PRAISE

It took me a while to learn how important praise is in my life. Because of this I have put a stress on praise several times in this book. Other important principles are repeated also.

Being tempted in the flesh like Jesus was in the wilderness will mature us. Again, we learn obedience by the things we suffer. It is hard to understand this but we must always trust in God. Our logical reasoning will betray us, but God's word will not. Sacrifice of praise is necessary. *Hebrews 13:15* "By Him therefore, *let us offer the sacrifice of praise to God continually,* that is, the fruit of our lips giving thanks to his name. [16]But to do good and to communicate forget not: for with such sacrifices God is well pleased."

If we do not praise God the stones will cry out. Luke 9:37-40 (Could that be the reason for so many earthquakes in these last days? I was in Long Beach, California, during an earthquake and I heard the stones cry out from several thousand feet below the surface.) Praise is in the Bible 2,000 times. It is a main emphasis of the Bible. Praise is taking God at His word. In the book "From Prison to Praise" living in praise was the answer to all problems.

Rejoice in the Lord always and again I say rejoice. Thanking God for what He allows in our life will keep our attitudes positive. Once we have proven it, we can believe it.

We think that to love our enemies is not possible. All we need to do is to start thanking God even for evil people and we will end up loving the one we hate. We must first confess our own sin, that of reacting negatively to the evil of others. This takes time but time is now on your side. Praise God for that evil person on a continuous basis and wait until God does what He says He will do. We need to hold on to what God says and not to our own reasoning. It is only proper to take God at His Word.

CHAPTER 14 DANGER WITH EDUCATION

The danger with education is that we learn what is good and evil, and we make the choice ourselves of what is right or wrong. Knowledge puffs a man up but love edifies. This was Eve's temptation, to eat from the tree of knowledge of good and evil. If we knew what is right and wrong in every situation we would not need God. But Satan doesn't tell us the whole truth. Satan wanted to be like the Most High God. His punishment for wanting to be equal with God was to be cast to the earth and finally into the lake of everlasting fire with those whom he had deceived while on this earth.

So when bad comes upon us, God's grace will have us overcome that evil with righteousness. God's grace will depend on humility. So the bad track is Satan trying to destroy us but God is in control where He will not allow Satan to tempt us more than we are able to bear. This whole system of temptation is under God's control. Satan needs permission from God in everything he does. Read the book of Job to learn more on Satan's limited power.

Learning by experience is much more than classroom knowledge. Just knowledge is not sufficient. The Bible says that knowledge will puff us up and love will edify, so knowledge without application is dangerous even if it is knowledge of the Bible. I have seen Bible scholars end up with bitterness toward each other after disagreements over what is right and wrong.

In a mission organization I saw problems with leadership in every country where I served as a missionary. The sad thing is, even in the most Spiritual Churches eventually leaders who started a wonderful missionary organization will have disagreements. There is much suffering when there is disagreement and no side wins. It is not a matter of who is right and wrong but a matter of conflict. When there is reconciliation, then a promise of God can become alive and we will be able to see the joy set before us. Each time we overcome temptation we will relate to Christ's sufferings. This is how the Lord has His Word to change us. It is not doctrine but the promises of God that change us. The promises are given to those who obey Him. It is God's love that sets this in motion. Remember, if we do not humble ourselves we will not start this process rolling. So much depends on humility. It starts with Salvation but it goes on to give us the power to overcome the temptations of Satan. Do not underestimate the power of grace to overcome conflict. But also do not think grace is all on the part of God and nobody will go to the lake of fire.

CHAPTER 15 TEMPTATION AND TESTING

Testing from God and temptation from Satan have a connection. You would have to agree that they both induce sufferings, and sufferings are necessary so we can reign with Christ. If we suffer with Christ we will reign with Him.

If all good things come from God, why is there so much suffering? It is suffering that comes from Satan and they come on the unbeliever and the believer also. Satan's purpose for suffering is for destruction. When one becomes a believer Satan's temptations will even have greater magnitudes. Everyone wants to be as the Apostle Paul but without the 5 whippings and being beaten with rods three times and stone and left for dead. On top of that Paul was in prison often.

When suffering comes, bad negative attitudes will have us fall into temptation. Wrong attitudes bring anger and will make one bitter. And that bitterness will bring others down with us. Then we will end up having a nervous breakdown, burnout, insanity, and self-destruction. If we try to live only on the good we do, we will be proud, thinking we are better than others. We need the bad to balance the good. If we complain when the bad comes the good will cause pride and the bad will cause bitterness. Doctors say that up to 90 percent of all sickness is because of bitterness. We need to thank God for the bad which helps us overcome the pride when good is blessing us. We can't humble ourselves by ourselves but God allows the sufferings in our life so we will by the grace of God humble ourselves.

The suffering of temptation and falling into temptation are two different things. Temptations are designed to bring humility. God resists the proud and gives grace unto the humble. When we resist grace we fall into temptation. Seemingly there is no obedience to God without temptation but obedience comes when we endure temptation. We learn obedience by the things we suffer. Sufferings are not from God. But when we learn obedience we must be willing to suffer. Satan

19

is strong in his temptations but once we get victory over the temptations the joy is unspeakable. Falling into temptation brings us into disobedience. Obedience is the principle thing in being right with God so Satan will continue in different temptations to destroy us from being obedient to our heavenly Father. Abraham started the Jewish race but even he struggled to be obedient in sacrificing his son. It was through faith (trusting God) that he became the father of many nations. See Genesis 17:4 and Romans 4:17. Isaac and Jacob carried on this faith. When God's people became disobedient God allowed their enemies to persecute them over and over again to this day. This has caused many Jews to leave their Jewish roots. The history of the Jewish nation is for our learning. If we do not learn by the Jews' disobedience we will be like them. In the last days this is what will happen. The Jew will return to God because of the Gentile's disobedience. The Gentiles didn't intentionally become disobedient but they didn't learn from the Jews' disobedience. Paul saw his necessity to suffer when God sent Satan to buffet him so he would not exalt himself because of God's blessings. God had to send the "bad" to keep the "good" from having pride. I have seen many stray from God because they couldn't balance out the good and the bad. I can talk about myself in that area all too many times. We need to look out for each other instead of complaining to each other. I think to myself that I will be learning these things for the rest of my life. Paul said, "woe unto me, if I preach not the Gospel." *1 Cor. 9:16.* Paul didn't preach because he was an apostle but he became an apostle by learning obedience of sharing his faith. Jesus trained his disciples to preach. The word "preach" doesn't mean to train other Christians in a building. The scriptures use the word "preach" as in sharing your faith in public. The word "preach" is found 139 times in the New Testament and each time

"preaching" is used, it is used to preach to the non-Christians in public. In the setting with only Christians the word "teach" is used.

Humility is needed for salvation but humility is needed at the start of each situation or trials we face daily. We have the ability to overcome temptation each time we humble ourselves. Through testing we grow in Christ and when we pass the test God will allow even a stronger temptation for us to grow in more grace. There is a connection between the temptations of Satan and the testing of God. The word "test" is not in the King James Bible. But God will "try" us and "prove" us, which I believe, is in the category of testing. We need to prove what God says by obedience to His Word and God will be faithful to His Word. If we think it is impossible to love our enemy, it is because we haven't proven it. But to prove it we must first confess our sin. The sin of not being able to love our enemy seems to be impossible to overcome—that is our own reasoning.

CHAPTER 16 MY BIGGEST PROBLEM

Does the Bible give daily directions? I have heard of people getting into problems over their head and after hours in the Bible they found a solution. I thought: is this the process every time a problem arises or could I daily find God's directions?

As I grew in my Christian life almost everyone convinced me that I had to read the Bible daily and we must be obedient to the Word of God. The problem was that I didn't see many Christians putting this adventure into practice. What I did see was that doctrine was the most important thing in the Church but that didn't give me understanding in resolving problems. Everyone wants to live by their doctrine but that only dissolves unity among different denominations.

Yet when I went to different churches that had different doctrines it appeared to be more in belief than obedience to what Jesus says. In fact no matter how many denominations I attended there was no noticeable difference in character. All I discovered was partiality. When I asked my pastor about different doctrines, he told me that our church had the best interpretation of the Bible. I wasn't really happy with that answer but I liked the pastor so I shelved my curiosity at that time.

As I travelled through the States the problem was multiplied. I was able to have fellowship with my home church but that was my partiality. In public I met other Christians who stressed their doctrine. Doctrinal differences only showed me a lack of unity in most cases.

After time I changed my doctrine. I started out with the Holiness movement, then the Pentecostals and then the Baptists.

My problem was I wasn't resolving my own problems so I decided to put my stress not on doctrine but my own personal relationship with Jesus.

The common denominator with all denominations was to have daily time with God so that was the way I decided to go.

As I searched the Bible I noticed that Jesus had an emphasis on commandments and said little about doctrine. Jesus only said: "My doctrine is to do the will of my Father." He also said to watch out for the doctrine of men and He criticized the leaders at that time, not for their doctrine but that they had no obedience, so Jesus called them hypocrites. This made the leaders angry and they decided to make plans to kill Jesus.

Jesus made one commandment more important than all the rest. In fact all other doctrine is hinged on that doctrine of love. It is in two parts, and they are to love God and to love others. They were both difficult to do in the flesh. To love God took away the things I enjoyed to do in the flesh and to love others I would have to include my enemies. The love I had in this world was the opposite of God's love. The Bible calls the love for the world lust. In Biblical terms it is the lust of flesh and lust of the eyes. Spiritually speaking, lust is the opposite of God's love.

CHAPTER 17 THE FATHER'S LOVE

James 5:15-16 "And the prayer of faith shall save the sick, and the Lord shall raise him up; and if he have committed sins, they shall be forgiven him. [16]Confess *your* faults one to another, and pray one for another, that you may be healed. The effectual fervent prayer of a righteous man avails much."

There are two ways of discerning this verse. The first is we can be healed physically and the second is more important, which is that we can be healed from broken relationships so we can come into unity.

This is the great secret in knowing God; The Father, Son and the Holy Ghost are one, and Jesus wants us to be one with Him. In *John 17* the Holy Spirit is in us to make us one with the Father and His Son Jesus. God wants us to be one with the Father and His Son and to each other. It is unity that answers prayer.

In John 17 there are twenty-six verses which mention the Father, the Son, and us, over one hundred eighty times. The prayer of Jesus tells us that The Father, the Son and His children should be one and we should be one with one another. This is why love is so important. Love is meeting the needs of others even if he is your enemy. Jesus loved all His enemies, even Judas who was the enemy within the inner circle. Jesus loved Judas until the end.

It is so important to love your enemy. It is the secret of having fellowship with your own loved ones even when they react badly to you. Unknowingly, loved ones can be our enemy just by our reaction to them when there is a disagreement. Whenever there is a conflict each side has an ownership in the conflict that causes that person to react and the other to react back. Do you see how Satan sits back and laughs?

Irritation can set in and there seems to be no way to get out of it. We must confess our irritation to God. Confession is the starting place for all good relationships. Bad relationships in marriage carry over to our children and then to their children.

To follow Matthew 5:44 to love your enemy you must keep reminding yourself of the promise and in time God will do the impossible. What is impossible with man is possible with God. It's not just knowing this verse but memorizing it so you can meditate on it day and night.

When we think it is impossible to love our enemy, it is because we are not willing to begin at the starting place of asking forgiveness because we are justified. This goes for any bad relationship that gets us upset. If parents would confess their wrong attitudes to their children it would resolve many problems. We can't love our enemies because we feel too justified to humble ourselves.

Satan has ways of taking control of our thoughts. It is dangerous to think our thoughts are our own thoughts when we are emotionally disturbed. Seek the advice of someone who is emotionally free from the conflict because he would be better able to understand the situation; they would be able to see your sins better than you can.

Satan loves to jump into our thoughts. That is where the problems arise in marriages, between friends, in politics, in religion and between nations. We think the other person is wrong, but without love for him we will only let the sin of the other be passed down to us.

The enemies of Christ killed Him, but that only released the power of God because there was love. God so loved the world for this reason. It was planned. This doesn't conform to our reasoning. No matter how intelligent you are, we can't understand what love is. Love goes beyond knowledge. *Ephesians 3:19*

Marriage on this earth can hinder God's spiritual relationships. Few marriages today have a daily time with their creator, using the Bible and prayer to respond to the Holy Spirit to give directions and resolve conflicts and problems as they arise. God's

love brings unity and the devil wants to destroy it by breaking down relationships, doctrinal differences, and not using the Bible for daily instructions.

Daily news reveals destruction all over the world. In the United States, sin is destroying the church by Christians not being obedient to Christ's commands. When the Jews became disobedient God had the enemy come in and destroy them. The laws of our land are our enemies but why? Because if Christians are not changing others, then others will be changing the Christian. Just in the past few years crime has increased 450 percent. We have so much new technology you would think that would slow down crime. We were doing well up to 60 years ago but the church has lost the zeal of our forefathers. Complacency means self-satisfaction and it is the opposite of self-discipline. It is so slow that we do not realize the change.

The problem now is cyberspace. It is not people going out to commit crime but they do it in their homes on the computer. It doesn't seem to be wrong because you are not leaving the house. New laws are coming into effect to combat this. Family relationships are falling apart and Christians are not united. People are looking for satisfaction from worldly riches and lust and wanting to be right.

CHAPTER 18 DOCTRINE

Christians believe doctrine is so important yet it is the cause of the many churches lacking unity. If one can't have fellowship with doctrines of other fundamental churches, they will not be able to have fellowship with people of their own church. To prove that, just about every church in America has had divisions because of conflicts within itself. And divisions continue to happen at a growing rate. The belief in doctrine has more emphasis in the church than obeying the commands of Jesus. That doesn't mean that doctrine is not necessary, but Satan uses it because doctrine is very important and that is why Satan uses doctrine to destroy love by bringing us into disagreement.

The only thing in the Bible Satan will not duplicate is the reproducing fruit of the Holy Spirit. Any false duplication can be easily detected and Satan doesn't want to reveal himself. The Bible says you will know them by their fruit. The fruit of the spirit starts with love. The love we can have is many times greater than the attracting force between man and woman. God is love and His love makes the world go around. When we have anger the last thing that comes to our mind is love. But our sin must be confessed before switching from hate to love and love never, never, ever fails. God's word tells us that.

Many times when I witness to people they want to know what doctrine I have. I do not want to offend them so now I am the first to ask what denomination they are from. That would inform me of their doctrine. If they are not part of a cult I can cope with their doctrine. As soon as doctrinal difference comes out it cuts off the spirit of love. If someone's doctrine is wrong don't expect changes immediately until you have proved that you love him. Love is the most important doctrine in the Bible. It is called the great commandment and the royal law. Find out if the person responds to love.

In a hospital in St. Louis, Missouri, a young good-looking nurse was leaving my room when I yelled out, "You need a marriage to take place in your life." She turned around immediately with a smile. I returned the smile and said, "Jesus would make a good marriage partner." Her smile turned to a look of disgust, and she continued on her way out saying, "I don't need Jesus or anybody else." She really wanted what she didn't have but she couldn't overcome her pride.

The problem Christians have is that they try to make others fit into our doctrinal position.

In the 1970s and 1980s the church had leaders such as Jim Jones, Jimmy Swaggart, and Jim Baker. These men persuaded churchgoers of their accomplishments but it was the government that proved them to be on the wrong path. Seemingly the leadership was better disciplined than the church. Since that time the church, to overcome sin, has made an emphasis on doctrine. If our government didn't enforce the law of the land the country would be a lawless land. Forcing others to obey the law shows no love. But self-discipline which is a fruit of the Holy Spirit is at least 95 percent more effective than forcing discipline on others. If the government could enforce self-discipline it would. So all the Christians have to do is to start changing our government by a Christian influence. It took a long time for non-Christians to change the church but slowly they did. Christians are fighting for Christian law in every way possible but by using the armor and weapons in Ephesians 6. The armor is the protection from temptation and the offensive weapons of the Bible are love and faith. Prayer which is mostly for unity of the saints, and by the mouth, to make the mystery of the Gospel known to all men. This is in Ephesians 6:10-20; it starts out by saying to be strong in the Lord and in the power of His might. We Christians need daily discipline from the Word of God.

Remember the first thing Satan wants to do is to get us into an argument. Satan can't directly destroy us but he gets us to destroy each other. The American Christian today is being persecuted by standing up for his rights. Christ came to this world with no rights and lived that way. Jesus came against Church leadership, not government leadership.

CHAPTER 19 THE ANTICHRIST

The following are some Scriptures on the antichrist. Not until recently did I know the true meaning of the antichrist. John said as he wrote this epistle that there are many antichrists. See below.

1 John 2:18-22 "Little children, it is the last time: and as you have heard that antichrist shall come, even now are there many antichrists; whereby we know that it is the last time. [19]They went out from us, but they were not of us. For if they had been of us, they would no doubt have continued with us, but they went out that they might be made manifest that they were not all of us. [20]But you have an unction from the Holy One, and you know all things. [21]I have not written unto you because you know not the truth, but because you know it, and that no lie is of the truth. [22]Who is a liar but he that denieth that Jesus is the Christ? He is *antichrist,* that denieth the Father and the Son."

The antichrist was people in disagreement with the church and as a result they had left the church. Almost every church in this country has had people who had disagreements and left their church and brought others with them.

1 John 4:3 "And every spirit that confesseth not that Jesus Christ is come in the flesh is not of God: and this is that *spirit* of *antichrist,* whereof you have heard that it should come; and even now already is it in the world."

2 John 1:7 "For many deceivers are entered into the world, who confess not that Jesus Christ is come in the flesh. This is a deceiver and *an antichrist."*

According to Saint John the antichrist is not one man at the present time but it will be in the future. See below: *second Thessalonians 2:3-4.*

The word antichrist is used only by John Paul's writings in *2 Thessalonians 2:3-4.* The antichrist may be the son of perdition, but now our main concern is that there are many antichrists around and many of them are in the church. The antichrist today is well represented in the DVD called "Time Changer." Christians are trying to apply the works of Christ without the name of Christ. Good works will never be sufficient in pleasing Christ and becoming a disciple. Christians in politics and business and in entertainment try to live the Christian life but are silent about making Christ known publicly. Most of them talk about the evil that is in our society and they want to make the evil known, but not the love of Jesus. Our society has so much control over Christianity that there is a fear to say anything publicly about Jesus. Making Christ known publicly is the emphasis in the life of Christ. Christ's disciples were taught publicly for three years. Why do we restrict the name of Jesus to within the four walls of a church building?

The Christian for the most part keeps his religion to himself. Even today as I was witnessing to a man he told me that he wanted to keep his religion to himself. I told him that was up to him, and walked away. He wasn't even a Christian. But many Christians do the same. In public they keep the name of Christ to themselves. The Muslims don't do that. Their main stress is to go public. That is why they are advancing and the Christian is retreating. In that respect we should be complaining about ourselves rather than the Muslims. Application of the Bible is seeing what is happening around us daily and receiving direction according to the Word of God.

2 Thessalonians 2:3-4 " [3]Let no man deceive you by any means: for that day shall not come, except there come a falling away first, and that man of sin be revealed, the son of perdition; [4]Who opposeth and exalteth himself above all that is called God, or that is worshipped; so that he as God sitteth in the temple of God, showing himself that he is God."

And there is a great falling away from the Christian church. Since 1960, about 70 percent of people have dropped out of the church. Christians want to make known everything our government is doing wrong but not telling them in love what is right. The other day I was talking to a gentleman who said that we need to know the truth. I asked him what is the truth. He said that it depended on the situation. I told him the truth must be the same yesterday, today and forever. Without absolute truth there will be only arguments.

Christians will eat together and have sports and hobbies together but there is not much Joy to enter together into a lovely relationship with Jesus and let Him be part of our conversation. This is a type of antichrist. It is not our job to tell others that they are wrong. We should be telling and showing others truth which is lasting. We are not to offend others. We should be preaching the Kingdom of God. Worship in church has its limitations.

All Christianity should be controlled by Jesus. He is the authority and everything He said and did will determine if we are obedient to His teachings.

What has happened since Christ ascended is that men made their own rules for the Christian life. These are some of the things that have happened down through history:

1. Millions have been murdered by church leaders.

2. Each time a group wanted to break off from the mother Church conflict was the result.

3. Because Jesus had the multitude following Him the leaders thought the solution was to kill Him.

4. Leaders wanted to use their power to control the congregation.

5. The church formed doctrines that didn't come from the Bible. Jesus said that they will kill you, thinking they are doing God a favor.

6. In the free world, doctrine became the principle of turning the churches against each other. Even the fundamental denominations have doctrines in opposite extremes.

7. Denominations destroy genuine love between the Believers.

8. Conflicts in the church caused lasting bitterness.

9. Jesus taught us to love our enemy which was so strong a concept that Jesus said even anger would be like murder.

Here are the most important commands of Jesus which should be priority. They are the Great commandments and the Great commission. The first is love so that there would be good relationships between God and man. The second Command is to share with the world repentance, for the kingdom of God is at hand. This was the primary reason for the first Command of love. Most Christians minimize these doctrines.

The multitude that followed Jesus were nothing more than followers but they were not the ones that reproduced themselves as Christians. Christ's disciples doubted Christianity even after the resurrection. If we do not continue the work that Jesus started, we too will doubt also. Who you love is who you will talk about. People say that I have the gift of evangelism which may be true but there is no gift of love. Love is the fruit of the Spirit. Nobody says that they have a gift when they fall into love with the opposite sex. God says: "we love Him because He first loved us." Love is an attraction to God and to others. Jesus says: "if you love Me, keep my commandments." The love in marriage can't compare with God's love. The Lord will give us this love for the asking. To draw people to Christ it takes Christ's love.

Young people dream about the opposite sex, read love stories about the opposite sex, and want that perfect partner to acquire happiness which nothing else in this world can give them but little do they realize that marriage is nothing more than the love of this world. Jesus said in end time people will be eating, drinking, and given marriage. Jesus compared marriage to Himself that we should be living as one but marriages as we know them will not be in heaven. God's love is so different than what is in this world. "... Anyone who has the love of this world is not of God." See *1John 215-16*.

CHAPTER 20 LOVE BEYOND THIS WORLD

There is no way to compare God's genuine love to what is on this earth. This is why God wants us to experience what it means to have His love. To love God with all our body, soul, spirit, and strength, including emotions.

Love in Marriage on this earth can hinder our spiritual love with God. If Christians do not continue their love for God together in their marriage they will not be a godly influence on others. Few marriages today have a daily time with their creator in using the Bible and prayer to respond to the Holy Spirit, who will give us directions and resolve conflicts and problems as they arise. God's love brings unity and the devil wants to destroy it. Every couple that I have counseled with marital problems said that their spiritual condition was minimal.

The Missionary Alliance Church had a research project done on Christian families. It was found that children of Christian families did not retain their Christian life after growing up. This also includes pastors' children. Many Christians do not think they are responsible for their children's salvation. Righteousness is handed down just like sin is handed down. In *First Corinthian 15:22, 34, 42, 45-50*, the first Adam started corruption and the last Adam, Jesus, handed down righteousness and eternal life. *Proverbs 22:6* "Train up a child in the way he should go: and when he is old, he will not depart from it." *Acts 16:31* "Believe on the Lord Jesus Christ and you will be saved and your family."

A married person's responsibility is bringing their children into salvation and that should happen within themselves before they get married so the process will continue. It is a long hard process but it means more to the Lord than your other ministries. For the unmarried Christian; his children are the ones he leads to the Lord and brings them into maturity. They are called spiritual children. An interesting fact about Paul's disciples: they were not his own converts but converts of others, like Titus, Timothy, and Tychicus. Paul was an evangelist but his main job was raising spiritual children and that is called discipleship. Discipleship is not a gift. God wants all Christians to be disciples. The first thing Christ said in *Matthew 4:17* was "Repent for the Kingdom of God is at hand." Then two

verses later He said: "Follow Me and I will make you fishers of men."

That means to obey what Jesus tells us to do.

In *John 6:35* Jesus says: "I am the bread of life. He that comes to Me shall never hunger and he that believes on Me shall never thirst." In *John 6:44* Jesus said: "No man can come to me except the Father which has sent me draw him and I will raise him up at the last day." Then again in *John 6:48* Jesus says that He is the bread of life. Then in *verses 6:51, 53, 55, 56*, Jesus repeatedly says they must eat of His flesh and drink of His blood, but they thought it was ridiculous. Finally in verse *John 6:63*, Jesus explained what He meant when He said "... the flesh profits nothing. The words that I speak unto you, they are spirit and they are life." Jesus was saying that He will die for their sins but the people still couldn't accept His words. Then in *John 6:66* the Bible says that many of Jesus's disciples turned back to follow Him no more. Jesus then turned to the twelve and said, "Will you leave me also?" Peter then spoke up and said: *Verse 6:68* "to whom shall we go. You have the words of eternal life."

In *Luke 10:1* it says that Jesus had another seventy disciples that He sent out two by two. In John chapter six, Jesus may have had scores of disciples but only the twelve continue to follow Him.

Parents in discipleship with their children have a difficult task. It is the spiritual bond between husband and wife and children that flourishes the ministry. It is the bond between a Christian and his disciples that flourishes ministry. *1 Cor. 6:17* "But he that is joined to the Lord is one spirit." If there's no unity with the people you live with, there's not much of a ministry elsewhere. Since 1957, close to three generations have passed. If Christian children would have continued being united with the Lord, and their children and grandchildren also, and if you multiply that to the number of Christian families at that time, it would easily account for 420 million more Christians today. But today there are 70 percent less Christians than in 1960. It staggers my mind. But that number doesn't include any new converts in evangelism. Apostasy is the fault of Christians and no one else. Let us stop criticizing our government. If we criticize our government, we must also criticize God for allowing the floods, earthquakes, and storms that kill millions of people yearly.

The Christians today are not as dedicated as Christians were in the past. Any missionary home on furlough will tell you that. That was the first thing I noticed when on my first furlough and each furlough after that. When a missionary first goes to the mission field he has an idea what the Christian normal is. When the missionary returns he sees the church below that normal. That gives the missionary the concept how much complacency took place while he was out in the mission field.

In *Luke 14:23* The Lord said: "Go out into the highways and hedges, and compel them to come in, that my house may be full."

The drawing power of God's Love is far beyond the love of this world.

Every Church knows that we are in the age of apostasy and they are informing the congregation of this. There is nothing wrong with that but the church should be examining itself as a congregation and asking the Lord what they can do. Each Christian and family must ask God what they can do. I'm sure God would show us through Scriptures. In the Book of Isaiah, God's people had many warnings but continued in disobedience and rejected the prophets. They were deceived as Christians are today.

Apostasy started about sixty years ago. Today we have the same percentage of people not going to church as the percentage that went to church back in 1960. In the late 1950s America had, percentage-wise, more people going to church than in the history of our country. Now we have less people going to church in the history of our country. The problem is quite simple. If Christians are not changing the world, the world is changing

Christians. Any returning missionary will tell you that they see the Christian deteriorating spiritually as they are being conformed to this world. That means the world is changing the Christian. We see in what areas our government is wrong and many Christian radio and television programs have aired the corruption on a continuous basis. And when Christians hear the news, they relay it to their friends. So the news is on everyone's back porch. Could it be that this may do more harm than good? To hear horrifying news has Christians complaining to each other, but they are not caught up with the present truth to see what God is telling them.

Our society is so corrupt. When Christians receive new information we want to make the danger known to warn other Christians. All Christians today know what is happening, but the conditions are only getting worse. All we are doing is spreading the bad news, yet we think it important to do so. I am not against writing our congressmen, but we have done that for years and the situation only gets worse. An introspection of ourselves must be made. We need to recognize that we are part of the apostate church. We should ask, "What can I do about it?" Since 1957 the world is changing the church. We should be concerned about getting the world out of our lives. Many church disagreements have ended up in conflict which resulted in many parishioners leaving the church all over America. People are looking for satisfaction by worldly riches and lust and wanting to be right and not being willing to accept themselves as wrong. *Peter 2.19-25.* Jesus took our sins on Himself. If I took the wrongs of others I would have nothing to complain about. But if I allow the wrongs of others to make me angry and bitter I would destroy myself. During the time period of the 9-11 attacks, most of us recognized that the spiritual condition of our country was not strong but it wasn't long before things went back to normal.

To help myself spiritually I had a slogan that reminded me to memorize seven Scriptures to keep me active in seven things. This was the slogan: **Bad Girls SLIPS.** Each one of the seven capitalized letters in bold print are for the following promises with Scriptures.

B – Build up myself. By my most holy faith and pray in the Holy Spirit. *Jude 1:20* But ye, beloved, building up yourselves on your most holy faith, praying in the Holy Ghost;

G – Give thank for all people I met during the week. *1 Timothy 2:1* I exhort therefore, that, first of all, supplications, prayers, intercessions, *and* giving of thanks, be made for all men;

S – Share my faith in public. *Matthew 4:19* And he saith unto them, Follow me, and I will make you fishers of men.

L – Love my enemy. *Matthew 5:44* But I say unto you, Love your enemies, bless them that curse you, do good to them that hate you, and pray for them which despitefully use you, and persecute you;

I – Immerse myself in God, not the world. *1 John 2:15-16* Love not the world, neither the things *that are* in the world. If any man love the world, the love of the Father is not in him. [16]For all that is in the world, the lust of the flesh, and the lust of the eyes, and the pride of life, is not of the Father, but is of the world;

P – Pray and Praise God continuously. *1 Thessalonians 5:17* Pray without ceasing.

S – Self-control *Galatians 5:22- 23* But the fruit of the Spirit is love, joy, peace, longsuffering, gentleness, goodness, faith, [23]Meekness, temperance: against such there is no law.

CHAPTER 21 RESTRICTION OF THE FOUR WALLS

To restrict this love to within the four walls of the church is futile for it cannot demonstrate the power of God to unbelievers. It has to be public. Our public example today is usually telling our officials where they are wrong. We complain when the Republicans and the Democrats are at each other's throats, but how much time do we spend making disciples? Disobedience is not doing what Jesus did. Go back to the source of Christianity and that is the Gospels. We have four of them and only one of everything else. The Gospels are not directly what Jesus said but we can compare the Gospels and look for what is exactly the same. That is where we should have doctrine. There are some things in the Gospel where the wording is not exactly the same and it can be difficult to understand. Nevertheless, all Scripture is inspired and can be used to visualize for daily instruction in what to do and not to do. See chapter 91.

The Gospel should be made public on a daily basis because it is in public where we have our jobs, schooling, and shopping going on. Christ trained his disciples publicly in front of the multitudes. We are so far away from following Christ's ways that it doesn't even seem possible to change it around.

CHAPTER 22 DON'T COMPLAIN

Jesus didn't complain to the government when even his life was at stake. When He was dying on the cross Jesus said, "Father forgive them they know not what they do." At times Jesus did tell His disciples concerning evil government leaders but He also told His disciples about evil spiritual leaders. The difference is that Jesus also told the spiritual leaders to their face concerning their evil. This is why it was not the government that wanted to put Jesus to death but the spiritual leaders who did.

CHAPTER 23 TRAPPED IN A BUILDING

We are trapped in a building and a building can't move, but the real church (Christians) can. Christ never set the stage to worship only in a building. That was seen in the Old Testament. Jesus did go into the synagogues but He was not well received. They didn't want Christ to tell them what to do. Church building started in the time of Constantine and most of the preachers at the time were educated men rather than saved men.

CHAPTER 24 PASTORS' KIDS DON'T SERVE GOD

Although people today put a great deal of money into wedding ceremonies, they want to get married for their own benefits mostly. When they do get married, they often have bigger and more problems than ever before. In a survey taken of pastors' families, it was concluded that few pastors' children are serving the Lord.

CHAPTER 25 THE WAY OF THE WORLD

In the day of Noah: *Luke 17:27* "They did eat, they drank, they married wives, and they were given in marriage until the day the flood came." Our format for love is eating, drinking, and getting married. If Christ is not in everything we do, the end will come upon us and we will not know it.

God compares marriage to the Kingdom of God because two must be one. In *John 17:23* Christ says we must be one with Him and the Father. *Revelation 3:20* states Jesus is in us and we are in Him. The King of this universe wants to come down to earth and dwell in us. That is a love relationship. Christ didn't come to set up his kingdom on this earth, which has deceived the Jewish people and made them so rebellious. Now the Gentile world is following the same procedure. We have many kingdoms under different doctrinal structures.

CHAPTER 26 WHAT IS THE LOVE OF THE WORLD?

If the love of God is not a blessing by increasing the number of saints in the church there is a deep lack of understanding what the love of God wants to do in us. We Christians do not need to fight for what we think is right nor for our doctrine. Love is

above all the law and the prophets. For the last 60 years Christianity has been on the decrease every year. Now there is less than 15 percent of our country's population attending church. Less than 1 percent of Christian families have daily worship in the home. Without God's love present, all the rest of our doctrine means nothing. The most important doctrine is to love God and to love others.
Matthew 22:40 "On these two commandments hang all the law and the prophets."

The Christian life is by faith, and when the feelings come by faith, it's a joy unspeakable, which is needed so God can use us to be a witness to the people around us.

Feelings are very important but they must be backed up by the Word of God. It is so much better to feel like we love God than just to say it, and it is possible. If love was only by faith, then faith would be more important than love, but that is not the case. Love is the greatest. *1 Cor. 13:13* Love also is above our ability to think according to *Ephesians 3:19*. "We need to love the Lord with all our spirit, mind, soul and strength, which includes being willing to die. It was by love Jesus died for us." Look at *John 15:13* "Greater love has no man than this: that a man lay down his life for his friends."

CHAPTER 27 FEELINGS FOR THE WORLD

Since there is no good thing in the flesh, Satan will have us dwell on the feelings of the flesh. Without God we will get our enjoyment of the flesh. So feelings come before everything else. Whenever a thought comes to the mind that seems to be joyful, there is nothing stopping us. Paul said that what is gain for me is lost for Christ. Yesterday I was driving home and a thought popped into my mind: "It would be nice to stop at the store and buy a chocolate pie." I had a craving for chocolate. The temptation was the thought and the craving for chocolate was the flesh.

Some time ago I would ask a question to other Christians and people on the street. The question was: Can a person sin, because of his sinful nature, without being tempted by the Devil? About 70 percent said no one can sin without temptation. And 30 percent said that a person can sin without Satan's help. The strange thing about it was that the most mature Christians and clergy would take the second position with the 30 percent. I don't think any of these people had heard this as a question before, but some of the 30 percent wanted to even make doctrine out of it. I think if people can get Scripture supporting both sides of an argument, it is not worth making doctrine out of it. Doctrine is to unite Christians, not to separate them. But questions like that are good for witnessing adventures because it can get people into the spiritual without offending them.

It is hard to say no to the flesh. But this reminds me of what the Apostle Paul said: "... what is gain for me is lost for Christ." Don't try to win an argument, it is too much gain for yourself.

Youthful lust is very heavy when seeing a beautiful girl. It is so strong that fellows will break relationships with other fellows over girls. When that happens, how can you say that is love? Paul said that it is better not to get married because you will have problems in the flesh. My opinion of that belief is because it is impossible to separate love from lust completely. In California I witnessed to one fellow in a shopping center. When I told him that God compares our relationship in Christ with a marriage, the fellow said, "You know, I was married seven times." It shocked me and I said, "Why did you marry so many times?" He told me that he couldn't live without a woman. I said, "Well then why did you get divorced so many times?" He was quick to answer: "I just can't live with a woman." That may seem comical but that is why there are so many divorces. Men and woman do think differently. It is God's love that attracts men and women. What I heard many times is that it takes more

discipline to be married than to be single. Many will not get the true meaning of that until after they are married. Another thing Paul said is: "If you stay single you look for ways to please God and if you're married you look for ways to please your spouse."

Humans use much of their feelings to love the world, which is not of God. The god of this world is Satan and he knows the power of feelings. When our feelings are connected to anything of this world it can destroy us. The things of the world are anything that is related to what you see, or learn in secular knowledge, sports, hobbies, marriage, and the list goes on.

Feelings are good only when the Word and faith is backing it up. When I was new in the faith I was given the illustration of a train. Fact is the word of God, which is the engine; faith is the tender, and feeling is the caboose. All three are necessary but in that order. Satan likes to have our feelings and emotions controlling us in the fleshly desires.

CHAPTER 28 FEELINGS UNDER CONTROL ARE A BLESSING

I have noticed something that happens when I witness. God allows my feelings to be the same as the person feels that I am witnessing to. This is to help us understand perception so we will not get into an argument. When we witness to unbelievers they must have faith to believe, but also they must sense our love. Asking God for love before we talk to people will make God happy and us also.

What is impossible with man is possible with God because He said we could love our enemy. Read Chapter 11 (My Independence). I had love I didn't know I had. Sometimes it takes a very difficult trial to have supernatural love.

Feelings are so necessary but there are two opposites that can go to extremes. Those are love and hate. If you get your emotions and feelings involved in either extreme you are in for trouble. See Chapter 41 Scientific Discovery.

Satan uses feelings to destroy love. This is why we must understand God's love. The word love is usually used in connection with the world. That includes marriage. Marriage is of the world since there are no marriages in heaven. God is love because the Bible tells us so. The big difference between the love of the world and the love of God is that the love of the world is destructive and the love of God is to bring everyone together in unity. That two may be one. That is the purpose of marriage. In *John 17* Jesus prays and then over and over again He says that we may be one with Christ, the Father, and with each other.

Feeling for God is very important or we would not be motivated. Love in marriage is to live with each other. Love with God is to have Him live in you and you in Him. See Rev. 3:20.

With Satan, feelings come first, then destruction. With God, feeling comes last, then eternal life. Love between man and woman is first lust because of beauty or attraction, but if the man and woman love one another, each must examine what is inside the other person. Love for God starts with a relationship with God in our spirit, understanding with the mind and disciplining our actions, and then our feelings and emotions will follow from the correct source. Our love for God must be completely separated from lust. Lust and love are opposites. Satan generates feelings in lust and God's love generates feelings from the Word of God. This makes us a new person.

CHAPTER 29 JESUS IN US

Jesus wants us to continue to do what he did. And that happens by Him living inside us. Jesus wants us to continue on where He left off. This is based on the Words of Jesus when He says: "Follow me and I will make you fishers of men." Before Jesus ascended into heaven He emphasized the Great Commission, to go into all the world and preach the Gospel to every creature. Love is

the most important doctrine and it takes the love of Christ to bring the Gospel to all nations. In every country I have worked in, the cults have more followers than all the fundamental denominations put together.

If I did not have moments of Jesus dwelling inside of me with Feelings, I wouldn't have anything to live for. I call these times a visitation of the Holy Spirit.

CHAPTER 30 UNEQUALLY YOKED

Many young people have such strong feelings about marriage that they will even marry a nonbeliever. Love in romance falls way short of God's love. God doesn't want to give us love, joy, and peace for our own pleasure but for His pleasure. God's pleasure is much more satisfying than the pleasures of the world. See Chapter 39. If a marriage isn't centered around God's love then the participants are ignorant of the facts why God created marriage.

CHAPTER 31 CHRISTIANITY NO BETTER THAN OTHER RELIGIONS

Christianity is no better than any other religion without God's genuine love. Love is something you can't retain unless you give it away. "It is more blessed to give than to receive." *Acts 20:35.*

CHAPTER 32 UNRIGHTEOUSNESS IN RELIGION

Organized religion on this Earth reveals much unrighteousness because it is not possible to organize something God is wanting to show us by living in us. God is love and having love in us should come out of us so others can see Christ in us. "Know not that the Kingdom of God is within you." That is the starting place, not on the drawing table. We have a righteous God that wants to communicate with us individually and we can make love with Him at any time. We come into obedience by us choosing His love above the love of the world.

Isn't it strange that sometimes when I feel discouraged I'll do something I want to do to overcome that discouragement, instead of going to God. God is just waiting to hear from me. Catholics and Protestants will seldom labor together because of their different doctrines. Doctrine many times is only head knowledge. The doctrine of Christ was to do the will of His Father. Jesus had only a few things to say about doctrine. The main thing Jesus said is beware of the doctrine of men, which He repeated several times. Jesus talks about His commandments: "If you love Me, keep my commandments." It is strange that most churches do not emphasize Christ's commandments as doctrine.

CHAPTER 33 MORE PRAYER

Jude says to pray in the Holy Ghost by building up your most holy faith. "The Flesh is weak but the spirit is willing." *Mark 14.38*

1 John 3:14 "We pass from death to life when we love the brethren." Love takes away fear and fear can be produced in many different ways of negative gestures coming to you or negative thoughts coming from you. Negative attitudes is Satan's way to conquer.

I used to think that the doctrine of my church is what is going to build my faith. I was right, as I believed what the pastor told me, it brought me into a good relationship with the pastor. But now after studying the Bible and memorizing many Scriptures I have some of my own doctrines. However, the only time I share it is with other people who have the same doctrine. Today in many cases it is doctrine that determines fellowship. Real fellowship is determined if Christians labor together.

The Bible says pray without ceasing. Talking to God is only half the dialogue. We need to listen and obey also. There are over fifty commandments in the Gospels and love is on the top and is known as the Great Commandment. There is none other greater.

CHAPTER 34 IS DOCTRINE WHAT JESUS WANTS US TO DO?

Why do we put man-made doctrine above what Christ tells us to do? If there is no application to your doctrine, then put it on the shelf. Jesus says that His doctrine is to do the will of His Father, which is in heaven. When reading the Bible, look for ways of putting it into action.

CHAPTER 35 THE CHURCH DOESN'T GO ANYWHERE

Jesus wants to be the church in us. The Gospel is preached today but it doesn't go anywhere. The ministry of Jesus was public and preached everywhere, with the multitudes following Him as He was training His disciples. The people are the church, which most think of as a building. To keep the Gospel in the four walls of a building is the most ridiculous thing any Christian can think of and yet we do it anyway.

The organized church was against the First Great Awakening because when people become spiritual their emotions control their behavior. In *Luke 19:38-40*, when the people saw the miracles Jesus did they cried with a loud voice; some of the leaders saw these people getting out of hand and they told Jesus to rebuke them. Jesus said that if He rebuked them the stones would cry out.

At George Whitefield's crusades the people were so hungry for the Lord that they had manifestations that the Pentecostal church accepted later on.

The crowds that Whitefield spoke to started to attend the organized church. But what happened was that, because of public preaching, the organized church grew and many more churches were built.

The Great Awakening of 1740 came to America because the Gospel went outside the four walls of the church. More men like Jonathon Edwards and George Whitefield are needed today. They preached publicly and demonstrated God's power.

The Second Great Awakening started public camp meetings that attracted people of all denominations. The organized church criticized the first and second great awakenings and I believe it was for the same reason the Pharisees were against Jesus—they were jealous. Leaders will be jealous when people do things without the pastors' consent. It is a fact in our history that these two spiritual awakenings for the first time took the Gospel outside the church. That was the example set by Jesus. Most of the life of Jesus was public ministry. If Jesus had his ministry only among the saved, the rest of the world would have no hope. Jesus shared the Gospel to the unsaved as He was training His twelve disciples. Jesus shared the same Gospel to the multitudes as He did to His disciples.

CHAPTER 36 SAME MESSAGE

Christ used the same message for His disciples and the multitude. The church does not need to prepare a special message for unbelievers. We are spending all our time and money preaching to the saved in the church and forgetting about the multitudes. I believe this is why there is a different attitude between clergy and laity. The clergy preach and the laity listen. This started in the time of Constantine. Constantine killed his brother and then his wife because they disagreed with him. The emperor had the right to do what he wanted with no questions asked. But his mother told Constantine that to make restitution he needed to build churches all over the kingdom and fill the positions of pastors with college dropouts. That is how the church became a building instead of the people being the church.

According to Jesus, a leader was to be the servant of all. Separation between the clergy and laity is not Biblical. If the clergy became the leader instead of the servant of all he will become a dictator. Jesus said the lay person should give their pastors double honor, but to the pastors Jesus said they were to become servants. It was the job of laity to give the pastor double honor and not for the pastor to take that authority for himself. And it was up to the pastor to be the servant of all. The qualification of the laity is to count the elders as worthy of double honor. *1 Timothy 7:17*. It would be easy for the pastor to think that he deserves double honor. On the same token it would be easy for laity to think they should serve the pastor. That doesn't mean that should not happen. But to forget the main qualifications of the pastor and the laity there will be trouble. A pastor has got to obey what God tells him to do and not enforce what God tells the lay person to do. Likewise laity must obey what God tells them to do and not complain when the pastor is not being a servant. Judas wasn't performing obediently as a disciple but Jesus didn't admonish him nor did He tell him that he couldn't be a disciple any longer. Jesus was a servant and loved him to the end. Jesus was called the great Pastor and He trained his disciples as being a servant. Pastors are not to get their educational credentials and forget about servant-hood. That is the world's way.

A disciple is a person who follows Jesus. Jesus said, "Follow me and I will make you fishers of men." That is when they became apostles and their job was to train disciples to start the process all over again. Salvation is only the beginning of a new life. In my trips through the States I didn't know how to grow as a Christian except to be faithful in going to church. So I attended church every evening for a couple of months, but instead of maturing as a Christian I wore myself out.

The best we can do today is to show people salvation and forget about discipleship. And if they want to be a pastor send them to Bible school.

The biggest debt the church has today is the mortgage on a building. The church is the people according to Scriptures. The

Saved need discipleship and discipleship is training Christians to preach to the multitudes where they are, in public. The church today is discipling less than 1 percent of the people. We see the multitudes daily at the workplace, at school, in the market, and at the mall. In many cases now it is unlawful to preach in public, but what made it that way? It is the world changing Christianity. That is what happens when Christianity is not changing the world.

CHAPTER 37 THE GREAT COMMISSION HAS FAILED

The book of Jude describes the apostate church in the end times. There are examples given of past events to warn us of the condition that will exist so we need to build ourselves up in our most holy faith and pray in the Holy Ghost, to keep ourselves in the love of God.

At the end of the book there is a plan to have us share our faith of the Lord Jesus Christ in two respects. The first is in love making a difference. The second is to save them with fear pulling them out of the fire. In *Acts 2:16-21* a prophecy is given of Joel that says: "And it shall come to pass in the last days, says God, I will pour out of my spirit upon all flesh and your sons and your daughters shall prophesy, and your young men and your old men shall dream dreams: And on my servants and on my handmaiden I will pour out in those days of my Spirit and they shall prophesy, and I will show wonders in heaven above, and signs in the earth beneath; blood. And fire, and vapor of smoke. The sun shall be turned into darkness, and the moon into blood, before that great and notable day of the Lord come. And it shall come to pass, that whosoever shall call on the name of the Lord shall be saved."

We have over the years slowly neglected the Great Commission to the point that church leaders have given up in teaching evangelism.

Are we spiritually blind to not see what is happening? We preach the Word, not that people want to hear us but without preaching there is no hope for them. God works in strange ways. If we are not sharing the Gospel with the lost around us each day, God doesn't permit the blessing of the Gospel to be in our own church. God works in unrelated areas. If we do not love the lost neither are we blessed being with Christians.

The unsaved coming to the church doesn't usually happen and when it does happen it would do more harm than good. Mixing the saved and the unsaved is like having the church unequally yoked. The same is true in a marriage. "What fellowship does light have with darkness?" Many pastors tell me that over 50 percent of their church are unsaved or not growing in Christ.

The sad thing is that the church is sick. The church knows we are in the last days, but the leaders think they are doing the best they can.

Our government thinks the problem is in religion and not in them. It is a fight, the world against the church and the church against the world. When there is conflict, there is no love.

Deep down, the church does want to change the world but there is no initiative to search the Scriptures to find out what we need to do. We live most of our life in doctrine with no application.

Traditions of modern day living have penetrated the church. We need to return to the beginning. That can be done by going back to the Gospels, we have four of them. We should study what Jesus did and said. Pick out similar passages from each of the Gospels so there will be no misinterpretation. When there is total agreement, put it into action. There shouldn't be any rejection from the leaders but if there is put the Scriptures into practice as an example to your church.

CHAPTER 38 DON'T GIVE UP ON LOVE

No one can give up on love because God is love and God has created us with a need for love. We think marriage will satisfy our love cravings but after our "first love" is gone the marriage goes downhill. God's love is pure and genuine and lasting. It is interesting to note that when marriages grow cold so does the relationship for God. When couples have wrong attitudes toward each other, they will have the wrong attitudes toward God.

The verse in *Jude 1:16* is a good understanding of human nature. Mankind will: murmur, complain, seek lust, lie and take advantage of others. And these are the things that are in the church today.

In *Jude 1:4* it says these people are the ones that creep into your midst, while you are unknowing. "For there are certain men crept in unawares ..."

CHAPTER 39 WHEN SHOULD WE FEEL LOVE?

You can't genuinely love someone until you know the person. In many marriages feelings come in before you know the person, which makes for a bad marriage. The same is true spiritually. You can't know God until you obey His commandments. What Jesus said to His disciples is exactly what He is saying to us today.

CHAPTER 40 THE FALLACY OF DOCTRINE

Today the church spends more time in doctrine and little time in application of doctrine. Both are important! You can't have one without the other. If you do, you do not have either one.

The Pharisees knew the commandments but didn't apply them, so Jesus called them hypocrites. *Matthew 5:20* "For I say unto you that accept your righteousness shall exceed the righteousness of the scribes and Pharisees, you shall in no case enter into the kingdom of heaven."

CHAPTER 41 SCIENTIFIC DISCOVERY

What you are about to hear is a scientific discovery of the human mind.

First, let's give a background. There are two sins that Jesus talks about where just the "thought" of them is a sin. Those two sins are anger and lust. They are in *Matthew 5:22 & 28:* "But I say unto you, That whosoever is angry with his brother without a cause shall be in danger of the judgment" *5:28* "But I say unto you, That whosoever looks on a woman to lust after her hath committed adultery with her already in his heart." The sin of lust and anger are triggered by emotions. These two sins can be secret sins. Secret sin is mentioned often in the Bible. The secret sin of lust can be kept secret for a long time but it will build up and then be exposed. The secret of anger is exposed by the one in anger, but in his anger he will not think he has sinned, and you can't tell him this without adding to his anger.

Scientists discovered what happens in the part of the brain called "Caudate Nucleus." When a person is very emotional in lust or anger the Caudate Nucleus releases a chemical that floods the whole brain and causes it to be glued to the emotional thoughts. You can't even tap off of the subconscious mind to retrieve stored information of the past. This is quite obvious when two people are in love, they think of each other day and night and will not listen to any advice. Anger is the same way. Your mind will control you and make you helpless.

CHAPTER 42 TEMPTATION

Satan's temptation starts in the mind but our new nature with God begins in our spirit. This means we must spend daily time in the spirit. There is a simple way of doing this: *John 4:24* "God is a Spirit: and they that worship him must worship him in spirit and in truth." *John 17:17* "Sanctify them through thy truth: thy word is truth." If there is any one thing that has done the most good in my life, it is meditation. If one is not meditating on

Scripture, he will only worry by thinking about a problem or something negative. During these times of meditation I have no frustration in my mind. Sometimes I have to discipline myself to do it. For example, this morning I had something demanding to do and I had to discipline myself to first memorize and meditate on my daily Scripture. That was hard but there was no frustration. You do have to use your mind to discipline yourself but that is a prompting of the Holy Spirit and not a frustration of Satan. What happens is that my mind now is subject to God's Spirit, which cuts me loose from worry.

No temptation is sin if it is immediately dealt with. If it is cast out, we grow in Christ. If the secret sin is repeated in thought, it becomes a habit. Anger is an attitude but the action will surely surface. With unconfessed sin Satan has control and he has seized the right to live in you. Our relationship to God is no better than our relationship with others, so we need to confess to others more than we realize. "If you do not love others who we have seen, how can we love God who we have not seen?" If we ruin our relationships with others we ruin our relationship with God.

We need to beware of temptation and be fast to respond. It is so easy to window-shop on temptation. We look at many good things, which keeps us from looking for the more excellent.

We need to realize that temptation is under God's control. *2 Cor. 10:5* "Casting down imaginations, and every high thing that exalteth itself against the knowledge of God, and bringing into captivity every thought to the obedience of Christ."

If a person doesn't conquer these troublesome thoughts, something happens in his mind that takes him out of control very fast. We don't normally think of negative thoughts as sin, especially when someone does us evil. We will not usually cast out these negative thoughts because the other person took an action that seems so much worse than our angry response. In *Matthew 7:1-5* it says if someone does you wrong and

you react, then you actually have committed a serious sin. The reason is that you will never be able to help a person in sin if you have a negative attitude. The Bible calls this negative attitude "a beam" because it has to be dealt with before you can help the other person whose sin is call "a splinter." Without loving your enemy that negative attitude will cause you to judge rather than to help.

Philippians 4:8 "Finally, brethren, whatsoever things are true, whatsoever things *are* honest, whatsoever things *are* just, whatsoever things *are* pure, whatsoever things *are* lovely, whatsoever things *are* of good report; if *there be* any virtue, and if *there be* any praise, think on these things."

Human love can turn into lust, and lust is never satisfied; yet that need for love continues. We can't live without love so we try to live with more in lust, thinking it is love, and it becomes less satisfying. God has love built into us, yet our nature seeks lust, which can destroy love. The driving force of lust is so great you can't even think of repenting because that one lustful thought dominates the entire brain.

Adam and Eve couldn't think of repenting when they were caught in sin but they knew they were wrong because they hid from God. Your mind is not under your control any longer in such situations. Not that you don't want control but the brain has taken over your "will." Now you become anxious which prevents you from thinking correctly. The world calls this being a schizophrenic. The Bible calls it a double-minded person, which is a person being unstable in all his ways. *James 1:5-9* Lust and anger are very dangerous just in the thought stage. But remember all sin is based on immorality, riches and pride. And lust and anger are tied right into these three sins of the world. A person has a need for love but when sin hinders God's love it is replaced for the love of the world to give us relief. *1 John 2:15-17* [15]"Love not the world, neither the things that are in the world. If any man love the world, the love of the Father is not in him. [16]For all

36

that is in the world, the lust of the flesh, and the lust of the eyes, and the pride of life, is not of the Father, but is of the world. [17]And the world passeth away, and the lust thereof: but he that doeth the will of God abideth forever."

CHAPTER 43 OFFENSES

Many offenses come from the secret sin of our thought life, and once offenses come there must be forgiveness. An offense that comes to you while in prayer, immediately before you finish praying you are to go and find the person and make an apology. The church overlooks offenses today and they build up until conflict comes and many are defiled. *Matt 5:23-24 and Heb. 12:15.*

Hebrews 12:15 "Looking diligently lest any man fail of the grace of God; lest any root of bitterness springing up trouble you, and thereby many be defiled..."

If offenses are not dealt with immediately you will excuse them but they remain secrets within you. Secret sin hides in us but will make us feel guilty. When Christ said that one of his disciples would betray Him, all of the twelve felt guilty. Was it secret sin of lust and pride hidden in them? They believed in Jesus but their relationship with each other was not sufficient even to know the secret sin that Judas had.

The Bible tells us not to offend others. *Matthew 18:7* "Woe unto the world because of offences! For it must needs be that offences come; but woe to that man by whom the offence cometh." What that means is to let the offense come to you and not from you. But, when the offense comes to you, be not offended or you will react back. That is difficult for anyone to do. Reaction is part of our nature. The offense must be confessed as sin before the next step of victory can be recognized.

Jesus said some strong things against people but remember when you love someone you can say things that you ordinarily would not be able to say because without your love they would be offended and react back to you.

In our court system today, lawyers get evidence to convict you and they will do it any way they can in order to cause a conviction. They are not concerned with offending you, because when you react, you become angry and the truth comes out. Judas told the truth before he hung himself. He said, "I have betrayed innocent blood." He didn't repent, he just told the truth. Knowing the truth and repenting are two different things.

CHAPTER 44 HAVING RIGHT DOCTRINE

Having right doctrine makes us no better than the Pharisees. Right doctrine kept the Pharisees out of Heaven. *Matthew 5:20.* Church trials should be different but usually they are not much better. Anger goes back and forth until there is a split. Most pastors are not trained to deal with practical problems. They are trained in the knowledge of the Bible in the classroom. Jesus trained his disciples in application. The classroom is sufficient to learn how to preach but that training is not sufficient in resolving problems. To resolve problems there must be practical experiences in loving your enemy. Witnessing will help you there, because people like to argue about religion and we can practice loving them by not reacting negatively to them.

CHAPTER 45 RESOLVING PROBLEMS

In *Titus 1:9* Paul is saying you should use the Bible in a practical way to resolve the problems that arise. That can't be taught in a classroom. On the job training is so necessary. You can tell a new employee what his job is but he has to be shown what to do to give him an understanding. In studying the Bible we're able to rightly understand concepts, but to have application of those concepts we must meditate on the scriptures and the Holy Spirit will show us how they connect to daily events.

A pastor's job is mainly to resolve problems. Problem solving doesn't come by classroom teaching. Paul wrote his epistles concerning problems and he learned these by daily discipleship. Barnabus discipled Paul for several years. After that Paul discipled Timothy, Titus, Tychicus and others. Discipleship is showing—not just telling. *Titus 1:9 through Titus 1:16* "Holding fast the faithful word as he hath been taught, that he may be able by sound doctrine both to exhort and to convince the gainsayers. [10] For there are many unruly and vain talkers and deceivers, especially they of the circumcision: [11] whose mouths must be stopped, who subvert whole houses, teaching things, which they ought not, for filthy lucre's sake. [12] One of themselves, even a prophet of their own, said, 'The Cretians are always liars, evil beasts, and slow bellies.' [13] This witness is true. Wherefore rebuke them sharply, that they may be sound in the faith; [14] Not giving heed to Jewish fables, and commandments of men, that turn from the truth. [15] Unto the pure all things are pure: but unto them that are defiled and unbelieving is nothing pure; but even their mind and conscience is defiled. [16] They profess that they know God; but in works they deny him, being abominable, and disobedient, and unto every good work reprobate."

The major qualification for eldership is found in *Titus 1:9*. By the Word of God one must show a man where he is wrong. Then in Titus *1:10-16* there are examples.

CHAPTER 46 LOVE MUST BE PROVEN

Even in a marriage, a husband must prove his love to his wife daily. Admonishing without love will do more harm than good. The reason why wives do not want to submit to their husbands is because love is lacking. No argument is won without love.

Notice the commands in *Ephesians 5:21-25* [21] "Submitting yourselves one to another in the fear of God. [22] Wives, submit yourselves *unto your own husbands* as unto the Lord. [23] For the husband is the head of the wife, even as Christ is the head of the church: and he is the saviour of the body. [24] Therefore as the church is subject unto Christ, so *let* the wives *be* to their own husbands in everything. [25] Husbands, *love your wives,* even as Christ also loved the church, and gave himself for it..."

I have seen husbands and wives go around and around with these two commands. The husband says his wife doesn't submit to him and the wife says her husband does not love her. They both may be right but each one is trying to enforce the command that God tells the other to do. If the husband loved his wife she would submit. And if the wife submitted to her husband he would love her. What happened was they lost their first love. In their first love they were both obedient to God's commands. Pure love requires that. God's first love ties a couple together but it will take discipline to continue to love when that first love wears off. It takes discipline not to react when you think the other is wrong. It fits under the command to love your enemy (or in this case love the person you think is wrong).

CHAPTER 47 PROBLEM WITH THE JEWISH PEOPLE

The Jewish people loved the law more than being obedient to God. That happens when one is strong on doctrine but weak in application.

There's no command to love them that love you. But there is a command to love all others, including your enemy. *Matthew 5:44* "But I say unto you, Love your enemies, bless them that curse you, do good to them that hate you, and pray for them which despitefully use you, and persecute you..." *Matthew 5:46* "For if you love them which love you, what reward have ye? Do not even the publicans the same?" After the initial stages of love, self-control is very much needed. There is no such thing as free love. Jesus paid the price for love. He died for our sins because He loves us. This refers to the Father's love in sending His Son; *John 3:16* "God so loved the world that He Gave his Son..."

CHAPTER 48 IMPORTANCE OF FAMILY MINISTRY

It is so important to have family ministries together. If a Christian family does not have joy in ministry together they will have their joy individually and usually for secular activities. Families must have spiritual times together. That must include talking to God and God talking to them. That means prayer and God's Word. Anything involving these two things is spiritual activity. Many marriages are over-involved in pleasing each other, meanwhile the partners forget about pleasing God.

Examples of spiritual activities are:
- Bible memory together as a family;
- Inviting unsaved friends over to eat and asking the Lord for wisdom to give them spiritual food;
- Having word surveys;
- Going to a restaurant with the commitment of witnessing to at least one person; and
- Praying together concerning each other's problems and finding Scripture for a solution.

CHAPTER 49 THE BRAIN IS NOT THE REAL US

Getting back to lust and anger. Lust will never have satisfaction. The more you lust for things, the easier it is to lose self-control. This can cause a man to cheat on his spouse or get into pornography. When a love relationship breaks up, the person will turn to lust to meet his love requirement.

If it is a case of anger, your whole brain thinks that one way and it will turn into bitterness. Even if somebody blames you for something you never did, that will give you even more anger because you are justified. Remember, your whole brain is thinking that way; you don't want it to, but it is beyond your control. When this happens you are not in control of the brain any longer. The brain has

control of you. Society calls this mental illness. At this time even self-discipline is difficult. You can't get your mind thinking about anything else. Maybe you can for a little while but then your mind slips right back to what is registered in it. The brain then tries to satisfy itself but can't. Lust will never have satisfaction. But the more you are lustful the more you want and the less satisfied you are.

CHAPTER 50 HUSBANDS AND WIVES MUST SATISFY EACH OTHER

When husband and wives cease to satisfy each other divorce can be an option, which will be the most tragic thing they been through so far in life. Then one partner pays alimony, which increases bitterness and causes insomnia. You will try to think of ways that will discredit the person you once loved.

But there is still a need for love so you marry again. It is so difficult to understand that God's love goes way beyond love in marriage. God's pure love can stimulate your feelings also. To love God with all our soul and strength means our emotions and feelings also. It is easy to have our emotions for things of the world because temptations are there to serve us in our desires. We must choose something from the Bible to emotionally motivate us.

When I first found the Lord I never thought I could have a joy in witnessing, but it was there for the asking. "We have not because we ask not and we ask and receive not because we want it to please our lust and not God." God's love will exceed anything this world has to offer but we must choose something Jesus did.

Lust and anger can lead you into the deeper sins of adultery and murder. Sin never stays at the same level. The final goal of Satan is to take us along with him into the lake of fire. The initial stage of help would be to praise God. It doesn't matter if you are a Christian or not. Praise can make you want to become a Christian or to be a better Christian. Praise is found in the Bible 2,000 times in the Old and New Testament. It is a major command. Heaven is full of praise. You would not be able to walk down the streets of Gold without hearing praise. But it will not be a command in Heaven. It would be nothing more than seeing the greatness of God. He is worthy of honor, glory and Praise. God's greatness is so much more than we can even think of in this world. *Ephesians 3:20* "Now unto him that is able to do exceeding abundantly above all that we ask or think..."

The next thing is self-discipline. The praises help get the brain to come back to normal and you can discipline your members to be used for the Lord. "As you had used your members to serve lustful desires, now use them to serve the Lord." *Rom. 6:12-16* [12]"Let not sin therefore reign in your mortal body, that you should obey it in the lusts thereof. [13]Neither yield your members as instruments of unrighteousness unto sin: but yield yourselves unto God, as those that are alive from the dead, and your members as instruments of righteousness unto God. [14]For sin shall not have dominion over you: for you are not under the law, but under grace. [15]What then? Shall we sin, because we are not under the law, but under grace? God forbid. [16]Know not, that to whom you yield yourselves servants to obey, his servants you are to whom you obey; whether of sin unto death, or of obedience unto righteousness?"

CHAPTER 51 ACCOUNTABILITY

Accountability comes by genuine love for each other. Loving others is the only way we will not react against them when in disagreement.

The principle ingredient for Christianity is "oneness." That means that we all think alike. It is like quality control. An example of quality control is using high tolerances for the product you want to sell. If you make bottles each lid would be able to screw on any bottle made for that lid.

In John 17, the prayer of Jesus was that we would be one with Him as He is one with the father and that we would be one with each other. That is quality control. A Christian should be able to meet with a Christian on the other side of the world and have God's perfect love for one another.

1 Corinthians 1:10 says to have no divisions among you but that you be perfectly joined together of the same mind and the same judgment. That means for everyone to have the same doctrine. Of course that will never happen. But if we made application of our doctrine it would be like following the commands of Christ. That means if you had doctrine that wasn't connected with what Jesus said or did, then it is doctrine with no application. Jesus said, "If you love me, keep my commandments." A command is an order that we obey and obedience is very important to be in a correct relationship with any authority that is over us.

Christians of different fundamental denominations that have different doctrines can be a problem. The best solution would be to change the subject. To say that you don't agree with our doctrine would enhance an argument. If it is a cult the Bible says to have no fellowship with him.

The Father's love enables us to do that. Three years Christ spent training his disciples in preaching the kingdom of God and they still had doubts, and even during the 40 days after the resurrection. About 400 of Christ's followers were told to go and wait for the Holy Spirit but only about 120 showed up. The purpose of the Holy Spirit is to join everyone together with the same spirit. The problem was that without self-discipline Satan would have control. We would all be perfect Christians without Satan. There is great opposition against witnessing because Satan doesn't like anything Christ stands for or for anyone that stands for Christ.

No doubt after the ascension the Christians needed persecution to see what God's genuine love was. There is something about persecution that helps Christians to love one another. Would God do something like that? Peter tried to question Jesus and he was rebuked. Suffering is part of life. If you do not suffer with Christ you will suffer for your sins and the sins of others. Jesus died on the cross for our salvation but we must see ourselves on the cross to suffer what Jesus suffered for. God will give us Heavenly love to do that. The love of this world is far from being sufficient.

When the persecution came the Christians loved each other so much that many nonbelievers came into the flock. And when public killing of Christians came, the people were even more drawn to Christianity. They saw how willing the Christian was to die, even with smiles on their faces. They had genuine love. Now, today's doctrinal differences will not allow that to happen. This is why sharing our faith In Jesus is so important. The only right way to be persecuted is for your testimony in Christ. *Revelation 12:11* "And they overcame Satan by the blood of the Lamb, and by the word of their testimony and they loved not their lives unto the death." This verse refers to the fact we are saved by the blood of Jesus and we are to share our faith and not be afraid to die for our testimony. We are not all meant to be apostles but to follow Jesus we must do what Jesus trained His disciples to do, and that is to preach repentance for the kingdom of God is at hand. Our government is becoming stronger all the time against openly sharing our faith. If you haven't been witnessing chances are you will not start unless conviction comes.

Soon discipleship was replaced with learning. When most of Christian leadership is based on learning, even if it is Biblical knowledge it doesn't give one an understanding of God's love. God gives us this understanding by personally being in us, but we must invite Him in. It is the greatest joy one could ever even think of possessing. Love passes knowledge. *Ephesians 3:19.*

Secret sin is mentioned in the Scriptures many times and it destroys accountability. Secret sin is what a person is constantly thinking about and it concerns lust

and pride. These two things make up the love of the world. See *1 John 2:15-16.* When thinking of these things repeats itself long enough the heart thinks that way. *Proverbs 23:7* "For as a man thinks in his heart, so is he ..." When a Christian thinks and meditates on God it is amazing what the Holy Spirit will do in us. Knowledge in the mind doesn't accomplish much without application. God wants us to obey Him. That is what application is.

The recent mass killings in our country started out with secret sin. There are two things that are out of control in America today: they are anger and immorality. They get out of control when one is thinking of secret sin continuously. On the national news I heard that a man thinks about sex every seventy seconds. And anger is so out of hand today that 65 percent of homicides are family related.

Being filled with the fruit of the spirit will replace the manifestations of the Flesh. The fruit of the spirit must be our way of thinking. In *Galatians 5* there is a list of both the manifestations of the spirit and of the flesh in the same chapter of Galatians 5. See below. It seems like lust and anger go together. Then in verse 5:21 it tells of the results of lust and anger. It includes murder.

Galatians 5:18-26 "But if you be led of the Spirit, you are not under the law. [19]Now the works of the flesh are manifest, which are these; Adultery, fornication, uncleanness, lasciviousness, [20]Idolatry, witchcraft, hatred, variance, emulations, wrath, strife, seditions, heresies, [21]Envyings, murders, drunkenness, revellings, and such like: [22]But the fruit of the Spirit is love, joy, peace, longsuffering, gentleness, goodness, faith, [23]Meekness, temperance: against such there is no law. [24]And they that are Christ's have crucified the flesh with the affections and lusts. [25]If we live in the Spirit, let us also walk in the Spirit."

Walking in the spirit is when our thoughts are under control. It is up to us to cast out wrong thoughts and bring into captivity every thought to the obedience of Christ. *2 Corinthians 10:5*

Remember Jesus says thoughts of lust and anger are actually sin. They become sin because that is what the old nature thinks about much of the time. I was sitting with a group of fellows and one of them said that he loves to think about girls. I spoke out and told him: "Yes, you sure can get much enjoyment looking at other women but it would not make you a one-woman man." I told him that marriage is beautiful and one of the most happy events in a man's life but divorce is the most tragic event that can happen. Is it worth it? In talking to people about the Bible down through the years I have seen so many people in love or fall out of love. Many times marriage starts out with lust and ends up with anger and bitterness. The Scriptures talk about lust and anger as secret sins in our thoughts. *Matthew 5:21-28* "You have heard that it was said by them of old time, Thou shalt not kill; and whosoever shall kill shall be in danger of the judgment: [22] But I say unto you, That whosoever is angry with his brother without a cause shall be in danger of the judgment: [23] Therefore if thou bring thy gift to the altar, and there remembers that thy brother hath ought against thee; [24] Leave there thy gift before the altar, and go thy way; first be reconciled to thy brother, and then come and offer thy gift. [25] Agree with your adversary quickly, whiles thou art in the way with him; lest at any time the adversary deliver thee to the judge, and the judge deliver thee to the officer, and thou be cast into prison. [26] Verily I say unto thee, Thou shalt by no means come out thence, till thou hast paid the uttermost farthing.[27] You have heard that it was said by them of old time, Thou shalt not commit adultery: [28] But I say unto you, That whosoever looks on a woman to lust after her hath committed adultery with her already in his heart."

Secret sin has already formed a habit before the action of the sin is revealed. Church-going people who seemingly have salvation are also involved in secret sin.

Church splits happen because of what is already in the hearts of the people who show their anger. Dwelling on secret sin gives Satan control and you can't override what Satan owns. Our mind belongs to God not the devil. Give no place to the devil. "Place" means when you allow the devil to have control of your thought life. Notice that sandwiched between the sin of anger and lust are these verses: Matthew 5 verses 23 to 26. To paraphrase those verses: When having your personal time with the Lord and you remember being upset with someone, make a commitment right there to see that person as soon as possible and ask forgiveness. That way you eliminate torment, which could be for a long time.

Matthew 18:34-35 "And his lord was worth, and delivered him to the tormentors, till he should pay all that was due unto him. [35] So likewise shall my heavenly Father do also unto you, if you from your hearts forgive not everyone his brother their trespasses."

In Matthew 5 verse 25 the message is to have an understanding in the future that everyone you meet must be an appointment that the Lord has made for you and we must acknowledge His presence as you are talking.

Time is something that can work for us or against us. It takes time to do things in secret, whether they are good or bad things. It takes time also to have secret habits form. Time does not heal your anger, it just makes one forget about his sin. Un-repented anger gives place to the devil within you. When we think it is forgotten Satan will remind you and the anger will come out. Anger is vicious when you feel you are justified.

But on the other hand time is to your advantage to grow in love. Allow time with prayer to build up your love. People that rip us off can make our human nature react with anger. So the first thing you must do is to apply a command of Jesus such as in *Matthew 5:44.* "But, I say unto you, love your enemy, bless them that curse you." We must confess our sin of hate before we love others. Your emotions will tell you it is not logical, but whom are you going to believe: your reasoning or God's Word? When your emotions line up with God's Word, then your body, soul, and spirit are working together saving the whole person, not just one part. The spirit is willing but the body is weak. Accountability is so necessary for maturity and love for other Christians.

First Thessalonians 5:23 and *Matthew 26:41* Our spirit connects with God's spirit to receive salvation. It is our job to transfer salvation from our spirit to our mind, will and emotions, which in turn must discipline the flesh or the body. The first time you confess your anger, you will not see a difference. That can be discouraging, but don't give up in what God has promised you. Memorize a scripture like *Matthew 5.44* and remember, now, time is on your side. Claim it and wait as you hold onto the promise. A promise is not ours unless we remain with it, until it is fulfilled. It took Abraham and Sarah ten years to have the promise fulfilled. Human reasoning made Sarah laugh.

Matthew 5:44 "But I say unto you, Love your enemies, bless them that curse you, do good to them that hate you, and pray for them which despitefully use you, and persecute you." If you keep meditating on that Scripture, it will change your attitude. They say it takes a commitment forty days to become a habit. I would never have known that if I did not try it. We must believe God will do what He tells us in His Word. This takes time. It may seem like bondage but only for a short period of time. After the habit is formed you are reminded of the promise automatically.

The government makes laws and enforces them. God also has laws but he doesn't force them on us nor does he want anyone else to force them on us. People have a funny way of thinking that they can force people to do what they say. Society can be that way, but discipline in the church is quite different. In fact, for the first 1500 years after Christ's death the church killed people for their disobedience. The church has murdered over 70 million Christians since the time of Christ's death by enforcing doctrine.

It is the government's job to enforce law not the church. When the church had the authority of controlling the government, it became legal to even kill. It's now against the law to kill people over doctrine, but different doctrine sure will get us in many debates and arguments which reduces love to that of the world. In Ireland those arguments turned into a war, which went on for years.

The person in sin must have conviction that he is wrong. And conviction comes with love. A good example is how Jesus dealt with Judas. When Judas rejected Christ's love, he didn't have anything to live for and we all need love to live. God made us that way and wants to give us His love inside us. We must allow the spirit to be in control and not our human reasoning which many times has caused division.

Today we have different doctrines that put Christians on different sides of the fence but the purpose of doctrine is to have unity. In *John 17* there are twenty-six verses that emphasize being one with God and each other. Satan tries to deceive us and does it by getting us to live in the flesh, and we do not know what is happening until it's too late because our actions seemed logical at the time.

2 Corinthians 2:9-11 [9]"For to this end also did I write, that I might know the proof of you, whether you be obedient in all things. [10]To whom you forgive any thing, I *forgive* also: for if I forgave any thing, to whom I forgave it, for your sakes forgave I it in the person of Christ; [11]Lest Satan should get an advantage of us: for we are not ignorant of his devices." It takes daily obedience to God's Word to understand the wickedness of Satan. Even Christians are unconscious of this, because of their lacking daily fellowship with God. Just missing one day is very, very dangerous. It means you have allowed Satan to take control for that day. There is a need to be united together with others in God's love.

A leader's job to preach is secondary. He is to be a servant in showing Christians how to live in love. A pastor's job is unifying the church and having the church in fellowship and agreeing together in one purpose.

Mr. "G" ripped me off but then wanted to make amends and called me up several times to straighten out the offense. I told him that I trusted him but he never did anything. For the next few days I was upset. My anger prevented my calling him up because I was not in control of my attitude. I then went over *Matthew 5:44* and asked God to take away my anger. I didn't see how God could change my feelings for Mr. G, so I claimed the Scripture to love my enemy. I let time go by. Then one day weeks later as I was walking past his place of business I felt love for him. This came as a shock but I then remembered going over *Matthew 5:44* daily. The promise was fulfilled just at the right time so I walked into his store by faith, trusting in God to do His part. I found Mr. "G" and I then told him that he had made a promise to me and he didn't keep it. He told me that he did his part. I just said, "I'm sorry but you didn't." When he struggled for an answer I said, "I have forgiven you and you need not feel responsible for anything. I shook hands and I left."

But I left with love because I was willing to take a wrong. That love followed me for the rest of that day. As I continued my day that love rubbed off on many others that I had witnessed to. I was so happy. Since that time I was set free from what that person did to me. The Bible says if you love them that love you, there is no reward. But if you love them that do not love you, that's where the reward is. Time can work for us or against us. If you are bitter, time will not heal your condition. But when you claim something you need from the Bible, time will work for you. God will live up to what He says. Our problem is that we do not want to wait for time. We want it to happen now.

Matthew 5:38-40 "You have heard that it hath been said, an eye for an eye, and a tooth for a tooth: ^{39}But I say unto you, that you resist not evil: but whosoever shall smite thee on thy right cheek, turn to him the other also. ^{40}And if any man will sue thee at the law, and take away thy coat, let him have thy cloak also."

The best help you can receive is accountability with another person you can trust and can see on a regular basis. Daily would be the best for this is the way Jesus trained his disciples. Accountability is sharing with another person of the same sex except in marriage. But even if you are married, a man needs another man and a lady needs another lady to be accountable to, because of secret lust and pride in the marriage.

Imagine what would happen if Jesus had a mixture of men and women disciples and they were together for hours daily. When a man has lustful thoughts, he might as well say goodbye to everything else. When I was a youth there was a saying: "Men should be in fellowship with one another, but when it comes to girls, it is every man for himself."

Pride can be dangerous for spiritual leaders. Because of their Scriptural knowledge pride can create tension with others. It is hard for men to get along with each other. Jesus had public discipleship to show them how to get along with others in public. When leaders fall, they take others with them.

James 3:1 "My brethren, be not many masters, knowing that we shall receive the greater condemnation."

Hebrews 12:15 "Looking diligently lest any man fail of the grace of God; lest any root of bitterness springing up trouble you, and thereby many be defiled..."

Accountability is where two men will give each other permission to tell where the other is wrong. It is almost impossible without acknowledging this. Even with permission to each other it is still difficult. I believe that the three years Jesus trained His disciples was mainly to accomplish unity between

44

themselves. Once any two men agree together they can have whatever they ask for. These are the words of Jesus in *Matthew 18:19*.

To form accountability will take a while. Finding times of being together in Bible studies, witnessing, and projects together. Accountability takes time and effort. You must be able to say to your best friend: "If you fail, then I have failed also." Only God can break that union; recall what happened to Judas. If Judas didn't hang himself the end would have not been as yet.

CHAPTER 52 PERSECUTION IS GOOD

The best time for the church is when there is persecution. An outside persecution forces men to stick together. Witnessing together also will bring persecution.

As I search the Scripture and pray I have a visitation from Jesus Himself periodically. It gives me joy to share God's love with others. Witnessing must be a habit in your life in order to train others in discipleship. Without confessing secret sin you will die in your sin as Judas did.

CHAPTER 53 DRUGS HELP IN FEELINGS

Drugs can make you feel that you are as free as a bird, but if you jump off a building you will fall onto the ground. Drugs work on the same part of the brain. To distribute the chemical throughout the brain makes you feel as free as a bird. Suicide is a great danger. The sensation makes you think you are in paradise. But to have the same effects in the future you must take a little more, which can lead finally to an overdose. Even wanting to withdraw can kill you. God created us to be controlled by Him and nothing else.

The choice is up to us. Starting at a young age a child wants what he sees. As he approaches his teen years, his brain and abilities develop and he wants so much more. At an early age is the time for the parents to start training their children in the Bible. From

cover to cover the Bible says disobedience is the problem. This goes for the children of God as well as for the children of parents.

A good way to start training children is even before the child has an understanding of right and wrong. Give the child a restriction of just one thing he cannot touch. Say "that is a no, no" and give a negative facial expression. That will develop the child's understanding more than anything else.

Break-ups in marriages are mainly because of secret sin and reaction to one another's behavior. If lust and anger are not confessed in their early stages it becomes more and more difficult until lust and anger end up in extremes, and many will be defiled. Then it is inevitable to have a church split or a marriage breakup.

Why are lust and anger so sinful just in your thoughts? It is because the heart of man is never satisfied. Finding a good thing is not enough, we always want more and more. The more we get the less satisfied we are. *Proverbs 27:20* "Hell and destruction are never full; so the eyes of man are never satisfied."

CHAPTER 54 JUDAS

Judas took several years to fill his mind up with lust for money. The Bible says that he loved being the treasurer because it was easy to steal. I do not believe that Judas wanted to kill Jesus. It was an easy way to make money. Why did he kill himself? He kept his greed secret for a long time, but your sins will find you out. When he was exposed and everybody knew what he did, there was no purpose in living any longer.

We cannot trust what's in our own mind, because without Jesus in our thoughts Satan will take control without telling us. The most difficult struggle is the war between good and evil, following us all through life. Stories in books, magazines, and on TV programs are based on good and evil where the good always wins. The Bible has this theme all through the Old and New

Testament. The good will win eternal life and the bad have eternal damnation. The sad thing is that only few will go to heaven and broad is the way that leads into destruction and many will enter in. See *Matthew 7:13-14.*

According to how Jesus dealt with Judas, the following may be a good way to handle sin in the church without having conflict. All Church division that I have seen in my travels ends up in conflict. Debates over a disagreement almost always end up having people taking sides. This leaves a scar on everyone involved and many times it scars the whole church. Being justified by what you think or even know what the Bible says, can become a chain reaction. Satan's favorite way to destroy unity is by having people think differently. All the way from close friendship to nation against nation.

Jesus knew all about Judas before he was born, so He certainly knew about his secret sin. Jesus kept the problem in the inner circle of the 12 disciples. Judas wasn't told individually about his sin but Jesus did tell all twelve of His disciples together that one of the twelve was going to betray Him. Jesus only said, "One of you will betray me." Since the other eleven had guilt thinking it was them, it probably relieved Judas of the pressure since seemingly the others were no better than he was. Under Grace it is possible to have secret sin in thought and action and still be part of the fellowship. In the Old Testament any serious sin met with death. Other sins were an eye for an eye etc. Finally at the last supper it was time to reveal the sin of Judas, and it was done in front of all the disciples. The other eleven were still ignorant but when Jesus gave the sop to Judas, he couldn't argue back because he was humiliated in front of Jesus and the others. Judas was speechless. All he could do was run away. This was the point of sin being irreversible, or the unpardonable sin. Judas was condemned by himself. Sort of saying, he had to die in his own sin. The following is a good example: I spoke in a church where a lady who was a board member committed adultery. She was caught in the very act but refused to listen to the pastor. The pastor asked me what he should do. I told him to take her into his office and share with her clearly what the Bible says. The pastor called her in as I was sitting in the hallway with a closed door. I didn't hear much of the conversation until the board member started to raise her voice. Very clearly I heard her yell out, "you are judging me." This continued every few minutes until she opened the door to walk out. All the time I was sitting in the hallway, I got upset, and as I continued condemning her, I sat there with anger. I knew in my anger I wouldn't be able to help the lady. I prayed, Lord I know you love her, why can't I love her? Then a Scripture came to mind, "You have not because you ask not." That changed my prayer. I said, "Lord I want Your love for this lady." Praying that one time didn't do very much so I repeated the same words over and over until the lady walked out of the pastor's office. When she saw me, she said, "Are you going to judge me also?" I said, "Do you know me? Why are you so angry?" She replied, "No, I don't know you and I am sorry for being angry." I told her that I forgave her and asked her if she would like to talk. We sat down and I said would you give me your testimony on how you got saved. She did and it calmed her down. I then commended her for her beautiful testimony. I then told her that I heard a loud voice from the pastor's office, would you mind telling me what that was all about. She said that she enjoyed our conversation and would be glad to tell me. To my surprise she gave me most of the true details. Then I asked her some questions. Are you married? Are you having an affair with another man? She agreed on both accounts. I gave her a Scripture concerning adultery, and she with a loud voice said, "Now, you are judging me." I said all I did was share a verse from the Bible. She yelled out again. "It was only your interpretation." I said, "I didn't tell you my interpretation, but you think I am wrong." I then said, "I will be the guilty party, please tell me where I am wrong." She was lost for words. I told her that I thought that she needed help so I told her that I would be speaking in the church in the morning and I asked her if she would be there. I still remember her reply, "You bet your pretty boots I will be there." I said, "I would appreciate you listening to my sermon but before I do I want you to judge me for my wrong before the congregation because I want to be right with God. I will call you up front and ask you the two questions about you being married and you having an affair with another man and then you take it from there, in how I was judging you. That silenced her and she picked up her purse and said, "I don't think I want to be a part of this church any longer" and she walked off. When I went back to the mission field the pastor wrote me and said the church began to grow leaps and bounds.

God blessed my love on her behalf. She didn't receive it but the issue was resolved without an argument.

Here is another example that happened in Winton, Oregon, but this time there was repentance.

Pastor Osborn and I formed a good relationship through a mutual friend, Bob Neil. I was informed that a brother was living in adultery for quite some time but he would not respond to the counsel of the pastor. He left his wife and started living with another girl and even brought her to church with him. Pastor Osborn and I shared the burden together and prayed. I was to speak that Sunday evening.

My message was on adultery and to my surprise this brother in adultery stood up in the midst of the congregation and yelled out, "I brought someone to church and people are talking against me for doing that." He was angry so I wanted to calm him down. I said, "Brother, if you brought someone to church and others are against you, then I'm on your side." It worked and he calmly sat down and I continued. "But did you bring this girl to church because you are doing God a favor or yourself a favor?" When I saw him starting to

get upset again, I directed a question to the congregation since everyone knew the man's sin. "How many love this brother?" I asked and every hand went up with a loud voice, "praise the Lord." Then I had another question and asked how many have been praying for this brother and again all hands went up. Now it seemed like I had control but it was not me but the church. I said, "Brother you may not have understanding concerning adultery but we are here to carry your burden. I believe one of two things will happen. You can remain in this church and let the people help you with your burden, or you can go your own way and you carry your own burden." Then I read Galatians 6:15 which explained what I just said. We then all gathered around him and prayed for him. The brother had tears of comfort.

The next morning I was waiting for the pastor in a parking lot and the brother in adultery happened to see me and rushed over to my car. He was so excited. He said, "When I took the girl home last night I told her that I was going to be a Christian and that she had a choice to make. Either you continue in the church and let everyone share your burden or you can leave and carry your own burden. She got out of the car and slammed the door saying there is no fun being a Christian and walked away with anger. Even though the girl didn't want Christ the brother felt the joy of Jesus.

When the pastor showed up and heard the story he was excited. The three of us went to breakfast together and we not only had good fellowship but our joy became the joy of the waitress as we witnessed to her.

These two experiences I will never forget but since becoming a missionary, most of the time I tried to counsel someone in sin I was a failure because when the sinner reacted to me I allowed myself to justify the Scriptures which only produced an argument. There were two things Jesus did with Judas to be an example to us. Jesus loved Judas to the end and Jesus didn't tell Judas his sin directly to him but indirectly He did. Several times in front of all His disciples He said that one of you will betray me. Today almost every church I have attended and even the ones I helped start have had severe problems with sin and have caused many to be defiled. *Hebrews 12:15* "Looking diligently lest any man fail of the grace of God; lest any root of bitterness springing up trouble you, and thereby may be defiled."

It is so easy for the counselor to lose his love when he argues. It takes wisdom and let the wisdom come from others also. Counseling one on one usually will produce reaction and you will end up with two angry people which will cause many to be defiled. Most all people have left the church because of offenses. Both sides will suffer: the person in sin and the church not being able to have the Holy Spirit take control as Jesus did with Judas.

CHAPTER 55 GETTING STARTED IN ACCOUNTABILITY

The church these days cannot prevent corruption but accountability can do wonders. In my experience of staying in homes of many families, I haven't seen many marriages where husband and wife have any accountability. Romance is the basis of most marriages. Basically that means allowing feelings to be the controlling factor. Feelings are important but should not be in first place in any relationship. Feelings can control truth, so feelings should be backed up with God's Word.

Our feelings must be backed up by the Bible before we can love God with our whole self: spirit, mind, soul, emotions, and actions. Wherever marriage is mentioned in the Bible, feelings are not a priority. In fact romance is not even mentioned in *First Corinthians 13,* the love chapter, where there is a list of fourteen characteristics of love. This is what accountability is all about. It is to control one another's feelings. A marriage without accountability is disastrous. Feelings or emotions are the main problems in

everyone's life if they are not under control. Your feelings must be from the love of God and not the love of the world which is lust. Love will stimulate feelings more than anything else. The love of the world will stimulate feelings before the mind has anything to say about it. When a person is controlled by feelings there is no self-discipline because feelings take priority. This is how rebellion starts. Lustful thoughts must be replaced by God's love which comes by discipline. Discipline is part of the fruit of the spirit. When one understands what God's love is, we find out that love and lust are opposites. The problem is with lust the feelings come first but with love the feelings are last. That is why discipline is so important. Again, Discipline needs accountability. In the Spanish language there is no word for "accountability." It must be explained. But the same in English—the meaning of the word must be explained but also shown. When two people come together in accountability the two must first share what has happened since the last meeting with each person being honest with no regard of their reputation. We do not like to share our imperfections. No one is perfect and yet the Bible says we can be perfect in love and love is willing to be wrong. The three main topics will be: immoral thoughts and actions, desire for money and things, and pride in reacting to others. Those three things will be the main issues in all of your accountability meetings. For the climax of everything in accountability we must relate to forgiveness and self-discipline. These two things will resolve the biggest issues. The hard part is getting started. When sin habits form in our life, humiliation will make a person tighten up on the inside. So prayer for each other is a must, before getting into the nitty-gritty. Too many Christians try to be strong in faith by keeping to ourselves that which will make us prone to have secret sins.

If we are not strong in our faith the world will take control. If Christianity is not changing others, others will be changing Christianity. The Christian population has decreased by 80 percent since 1957, so who is changing who?

Someone coming into a change by receiving Jesus is just the start. Change by being accountable is necessary to mature and grow as a Christian. This is why church is necessary, but church is not a building but a group of people coming together and being accountable to each other.

CHAPTER 56 LAW ENFORCEMENT IS GOOD

Without laws our country would be corrupt. God looks on us the same way. If we do not obey God's laws we will be corrupted also. Our government enforces the laws of our country. The laws of God are enforced only by God-fearing people in self-discipline. Is it any wonder that many backslide? They do not want to be the source of taking away their own sinful pleasures. It takes self-discipline. God says we need to love our enemy.

Proverbs 3:5-6 [5] "Trust in the LORD with all thine heart; and lean not unto thine own understanding. [6] In all thy ways acknowledge him, and he shall direct thy paths."

CHAPTER 57 THE SONG OF SOLOMON

The Song of Solomon is also called the "Song of Songs" because it was the best of Solomon's writings, and on that scholars have agreed. There is nothing spiritual in the book, but through an allegory the book becomes spiritually alive. The book has many interpretations but there is one thing all can agree with and that is: it is a love story. It shows how God's love attracts a man and a woman together in matrimony. The allegory has a spiritual understanding of how God's love attracts His creation in a love relationship with Christ that will change us forever. The love in marriage on this earth is just a small representation of the Father's love toward those who are attracted to His spiritual power that draws all to Him.

John 6:44 "No man can come to me, except the Father, which hath sent me, draw him: and I will raise him up at the last day." *John 12:32* "And I, if I be lifted up from the earth, will draw all men unto me."

CHAPTER 59 THE EARLY CHRISTIANS

Acts 2:42-46 [42] "And they continued steadfastly in the apostles' doctrine and fellowship, and in breaking of bread, and in prayers. [43] And fear came upon every soul: and the apostles did many wonders and signs. [44] And all that believed were together, and had all things common; [45] And sold their possessions and goods, and parted them to all men, as every man had need. [46] And they, continuing daily with one accord in the temple, and breaking bread from house to house, did eat their meat with gladness and singleness of heart,"

CHAPTER 60 GO AND TELL NO ONE

When Jesus healed people, He would tell them to go and tell no one. We should tell the world about the love of God; to tell someone of the good we received is bragging. When someone receives an inheritance, or a new home or car, he wants to brag about it, which only makes others jealous. Jesus doesn't want us to brag about Him but Jesus is looking for people to obey Him. Followers of Jesus want the benefits. Disciples of Jesus are willing to obey even in suffering.

CHAPTER 60 CAIN JEALOUS OF ABEL

Cain was jealous of Abel because Abel's sacrifice was better. The Pharisees were jealous of Jesus because everyone was following Christ.

The story of the prodigal son is the same way. When he repented, the other brother was jealous. Whenever someone receives something we want, what happens?

CHAPTER 61 FEW BECOME DISCIPLES

Very few of the people who were healed became disciples. They were only followers because of the miracles. Most of the church today is a follower. Followers will brag about their doctrine, or about their church. That is not being a disciple.

CHAPTER 62 SELF-CONTROL FOR YOU AND YOUR CHILDREN

Self-control is part of the Fruit of the Spirit, which is discipline. A disciple is a disciplined person. It is the only way parents teach their children to obey. And God uses the same methods on His children. Suffering is connected to obedience. Even Jesus learned obedience by the things He suffered. Why? Because he was human, also to show us exactly what we must go through. Suffering on the cross was by obedience. This is compared to dying to self, which is the second Beatitude. He pleaded to His father to take this cup from Him because He was human and subject to every temptation as we are. Jesus knew that He would have to suffer before He would have the joy. But He visualized that joy even before the cross.

Hebrews 12:1- 4 [2] "Looking unto Jesus the author and finisher of our faith; who for the joy that was set before him endured the cross, despising the shame, and is set down at the right hand of the throne of God. [3] For consider him that endured such contradiction of sinners against himself, lest you be wearied and faint in your minds. [4] You have not yet resisted unto blood, striving against sin."

CHAPTER 63 HUSBANDS AND WIVES NEED GOD'S LOVE

Husbands and wives should use the Bible to resolve worry. When two agree on the Truth together there is a oneness that nothing else can give you. This will put them in the same spirit. When the two people agree on what God is saying from the Word, then the two become one spirit and whatever you pray for, it will come to pass.

Less than 1 percent of Christian families do this. It is no wonder Satan has a heyday. The unnecessary problems in marriage are because of *not* having spiritual fellowship. Secret thoughts come when you get irritated with each other and think about the irritation. At least once a day husbands and wives should have spiritual fellowship and confess secret thoughts.

CHAPTER 64 SATAN USES DAILY CONFLICTS TO DESTROY US

Satan uses these daily events to cause conflict for us, but the Lord has a different purpose for these conflicts and He uses Satan's deceptions for our advantage. We have to see our need for God in everything we say and do. Christians walk through life in a lot of deception by not having daily Spiritual direction through the Scriptures.

As I look back on my own life, there have been many wasted years. Satan has a direct contact to our minds, by temptation, and he will reign there as long as he can. Satan not only puts wrong thoughts into our mind but he can also have us retain these thoughts as secret sins. Does Satan know what we are thinking? If he gave us the thought, he sure does. At the same time he will make us think there is nothing wrong in our Christian life. His power is greater than we can understand without God's help.

CHAPTER 65 JESUS NEEDED TO GO AWAY

John 14:28 "You have heard how I said unto you, I go away, and come again unto you. If you loved me, you would rejoice, because I said, I go unto the Father: for my Father is greater than I." The main function of Jesus coming the first time was to have His disciples duplicate everything He did and said. We are to be like Christ in every way by the direction of the Holy Spirit. So the all-time question when facing a difficult situation is: WWJD. What Would Jesus Do?

But to be like the Father is far beyond our understanding. Lucifer was turned down when requesting to be like the Most High God. Lucifer then rebelled with one third of the angels and started a war in heaven but was defeated.

This is why Jesus had limited capabilities on earth. "My Father is greater than I." We can do all that Jesus did but not the Father. The Father's power is beyond imagination. That is why He is worthy of praise. When there is no solution to a problem, praise God.

One day, years ago, I wanted to see how many times I could praise God in one day, so for each incident that I praised Him, I wrote on a card. At the end of the day I was anxious to count the number of times I praised God. As I studied the list I was astonished not at how many times I praised God, but because each time it happened was when something went wrong.

It showed me that when things go well the thought of praise is not there. Conclusion! There are many more opportunities to mature in Christ when problems arise.

Satan's punishment was to get partially what he wanted. He became god, but the god of this world. With this great power he tries constantly to deceive us to be equal to God. Satan wants to be like the most High but God wasn't pleased with that. What Satan couldn't be, he tries to make us to be. If we were like God we would not need a savior. The pride that we deal with in life is all hinged on the fact that we are "God," meaning we believe we are right and others are wrong. All that attitude creates is war in your relationships with others.

CHAPTER 66 JUSTIFIED WARS

We call it justified war because both sides think they are right. We think we can prove we are right by going to war. Reacting to others when we think we are right can bring war with two individuals or two nations. Jesus was not against a person being a soldier in the army because He knew what human nature will do. Jesus didn't condemn the Romans for having an army but Jesus was careful not to have his disciples to be in conflict. Grace is given by God to overcome reaction to our enemy. This will determine if you really have love.

In the Revolutionary War, England thought they were justified because they were the mother nation and the Colonies were disobedient. Of course, the justification of the colonies was in a different area. It resulted in war.

I often wondered if only I didn't justify myself, what would happen. I can't correct my past but I can remember my past sins for future decisions. If we do not learn from past sins, they will be repeated. All my conflicts was because I had reacted. Jesus died on the cross to show us that we have to be willing to take wrong. 1 Peter 2:19-25.

America has had many justified wars since the Revolutionary War and we are still having them. Especially since Christianity hasn't been much of an influence any longer in making the laws of our country. We used to, when 70 percent of our population were Christians. Now close to 80 percent do not attend church. Is that the government's fault?

CHAPTER 67 GOD GIVES US ENDURANCE AND PURPOSE

1 John 2:15 "Love not the world, neither the things *that are* in the world. If any man loves the world, the love of the Father is not in him." In heaven The Father's love will wipe away all tears from our eyes once and forever. *Revelation 21:4-5* "And God shall wipe away all tears from their eyes; and there shall be no more death, neither sorrow, nor crying, neither shall there be any more pain: for the former things are passed away. ⁵And he that sat upon the throne said, Behold, I make all things new."

Many people want marriage because it is the greatest love they know. Many times I have seen Christians wanting to marry non-Christians. God has given everyone an attraction for the opposite gender; when the attraction turns into romance we run away with our feelings, not understanding the Father's love is so much greater. It is difficult to think about Jesus when one is in a romance. We have a one-track mind also when anger comes into our mind.

There is a great need to study the Father's love. The Father's love is what we all will have in Heaven. Romance is deceiving. You cannot compare romance with God's love. There is no romance in heaven. The Father's love will be so much better. We can compare marriage with our relationship with God in that two will be one. Jesus wants to be one with us. *John 17:21*

It will be the Father on the Throne in Heaven and Jesus will be on His right hand where He is now making intercession for us. *Romans 8:33* "It is Christ that died, yea rather, that is risen again, who is even at the right hand of God, who also makes intercession for us."

CHAPTER 68 GENUINE LOVE IS BEYOND OUR UNDERSTANDING

On this earth we have no idea how great the love of the Father will be unless we want it more than anything else. Human nature thinks that marriage would be the greatest love, but in heaven there will be no need for marriage. God invented human marriage only for this earth. Most humans can't think that way. If one marriage doesn't work, a wife replacement is the only solution, yet many times they remarry against God's written law.

CHAPTER 69 THE NEW NATURE MUST PERFORM

Our new nature must be put into practice, privately and publicly in obedience to the commands of Jesus. Without keeping God's commands we will have an inappropriate understanding of God.

CHAPTER 70 MIRACLES HAPPEN IN DISOBEDIENCE

Because of disobedience, God's chosen people wandered in the wilderness for forty years and they are still wandering. The Scribes and the Pharisees knew the law as well as the best, but unless our righteousness exceed the righteous of the Scribes and the Pharisees we will in no wise enter into the kingdom of heaven. Matthew 5:20
Luke 8:16-17 "No man, when he hath lighted a candle, covers it with a vessel, or puts it under a bed; but sets it on a candlestick, that they which enter in may see the light. [17] For nothing is secret that shall not be made manifest; neither anything hid, that shall not be known and come abroad."

God allowed miracles to happen in my life as I took my first trip through the States. This was not to show me I was in obedience but so I wouldn't be discouraged in the struggles that God uses to have me be obedient. We learn obedience by the things we suffer.

CHAPTER 71 SECRET SIN

The apostate church may be the hidden sin in many church people. Satan remains in our secret sins but always looks for opportunities to surface them. They can be as strongholds even in the Christian life. *2 Cor. 10:4* "For the weapons of our warfare are not carnal, but mighty through God to the pulling down of strong holds ..." The Kingdom of God is within us but that can be of no effect without a commitment to the Lord.

Most people think secrets are wrong. But really they can be right as much as they are wrong, depending on whether the secret involves being righteous or evil. The secret of being more like Christ is not telling others how much you pray, in giving alms, or in fasting. That should be kept in secret. The understanding of being evil is falling into temptation. This should not be a secret, but it must be confessed as sin. This may not seem to be significant but the first eighteen verses of *Matthew 6* talk about these righteous secrets.

These good secrets are in *Matthew 6:3-18*, and there are bad secrets. *Psalms 44:21* "Shall not God search this out? For he knows the secrets of the heart."

The bad secrets start in our mind and the good ones start in our spirit. Both good and bad will be revealed. *Mark 4:22* "For there is nothing hid, which shall not be manifested; neither was anything kept secret, but that it should come abroad."

Matthew 6:3-4 "But when thou doest alms, let not thy left hand know what thy right hand doeth: *4 That thine alms may be in secret: and thy Father which sees in secret himself shall reward thee openly."* (This secret also goes for prayer and fasting, also in Matthew 6:5-18.)

It is difficult not to tell people about the good secrets that God tells us not to tell anyone, because we want others to know how good we are. That is pride. To the other extreme, God wants us to confess the bad secrets, which is very difficult for us to do because we don't want others to know how bad we are. That is pride also. In both cases it is pride, because human nature is contrary to God's Word.

A great man knows he is not God and the greater he becomes, the more he knows it. Satan wanted to be equal with God. He lost the battle but tries to make us be winners. That's deception.

A person who rejects God will have knowledge to fortify his belief in what he thinks is truth, and the more he studies the more he will believe he has the truth. Actually that person is making himself God by being deceived by Satan. Satan's fall was from desiring to be like the Most High. Found in *Isaiah 14:14*.

CHAPTER 72 THE KINGDOM OF GOD IS IN YOU

Luke 17:20-21 "And when he was demanded of the Pharisees, when the kingdom of God should come, he answered them and said, The kingdom of God cometh not with observation: 21Neither shall they say, Lo here! Or, lo there! For, behold, the kingdom of God is within you."

This is why it is important to find out who is who. We would be amazed at how many times Satan takes control of our thoughts, words, and actions.

CHAPTER 73 NOT A BATTLE UNTIL DESPERATION

Satan's temptations are not even a battle until we become desperate to want God. We either do what we want to do or what Jesus would have us do, and yet we fight within ourselves constantly with no understanding of what is happening.

In *John 5:19* Jesus says, "The Son can't do anything of Himself." Jesus received everything he did from His Father. When we make up our own mind we are not receiving of the Father.

We have a choice to choose God, and if we do not, Satan takes over without us even choosing him. We try to avoid suffering but we can't. If we do not suffer for what is right we will suffer for our own sin or the sins of others.

CHAPTER 74 SUFFER WITH CHRIST

1 Peter 2:20 "For what glory is it, if, when you be buffeted for your faults, you shall take it patiently? But if, when you do well, and suffer for it, you take it patiently, this is acceptable with God."

Our goal is to suffer with Christ in doing what he showed his disciples so we will become one with Christ.

CHAPTER 75 PERFECT IN ONE

John 17:13 "I in them, and thou in me, that they may be made perfect in one; and that the world may know that thou hast sent me, and hast loved them, as thou hast loved me."

We suffer with Christ by being a witness for Him. *Matthew 5:11-12* "Blessed are ye, when men shall revile you, and persecute you, and shall say all manner of evil against you falsely, for my sake. [12] Rejoice, and be exceeding glad: for great is your reward in heaven: for so persecuted they the prophets which were before you."

We need to be salt and light. *Matt 5:12-16* "If we suffer with Christ we will reign with Him." It wasn't just for the 12 Disciples of Christ, but for the many that would be disciples until Christ comes again. A disciple is not a pastor but a pastor starts out by being a disciple, and when he becomes a pastor he must disciple others, not just preach to others. Preaching is not discipleship unless we teach others how to be disciples. At that point your name changes from being a disciple to being an apostle.

Many pastors before entering into their ministry never know discipleship, so they do not know how to disciple others. All they know is classroom knowledge which is good for preaching, but not for making disciples or resolving church problems.

CHAPTER 76 TWO TYPES OF FOLLOWERS

It was the disciples who Jesus was teaching how to speak to the multitudes to make disciples. We still have the same Christ today to do the same job. Jesus had two types of followers. First the multitudes, which were attracted to Christ by the miracles. And the second were the disciples, who were the few who wanted to be like Christ in practical experience. The church today is filled with the multitudes and few disciples. In *John chapter six* Jesus was talking to the multitudes wanting to recruit new disciples when He said, "Except you eat of my flesh and drink of my blood you have no part of me." Before that time Jesus had seventy disciples but they left and Jesus was back to the original twelve.

CHAPTER 77 TOO HARD TO RECEIVE

Jesus told His disciples several times but it was too hard for them to receive, so Jesus explained what He meant in John 6:63. He said that the flesh has no value but He came in the flesh to give them the word of God. *John 6:63* "It is the spirit that quickens; the flesh profits nothing: the words that I speak unto you, they are spirit, and they are life." They heard the interpretation but they couldn't overcome their offense so they turned away. Jesus then turned to the 12 disciples and said will you leave me also? That was when Peter spoke up: *John 6:64-68* "For Jesus knew from the beginning who they were that believed not, and who should betray him. [65] And he said, therefore said I unto you, that no man can come unto me, except it were given unto him of my Father. [66] From that time many of his disciples went back, and walked no more with him. [67] Then said Jesus unto the twelve, Will you also go away? [68] Then Simon Peter answered him, Lord, to whom shall we go? Thou hast the words of eternal life."

Many elders today have given up hope in teaching evangelism. It must be the same reason now as then. Jesus said the harvest is ripe but there are few laborers. The love for the world was so strong that they didn't see the Father's love in doing what Jesus did in training disciples publicly.

Not many like to turn out for church evangelism. It just seems to be an unlovable church function. I don't believe that evangelism should be a separate function of discipleship. Anyone who gets into the ministry should have a love for evangelism.

Discipleship is spending much of your time together in public with other people. For example: Have coffee together, take trips together, and shop together. Do all these things as you make Christ known to others. I was in the library yesterday. I walked up to a gentleman and asked him if he came to the library often. That got into a conversation which we both enjoyed. I told him that Jesus was right there with us. For the next 30 minutes the man realized that Jesus was there. As quick as I walked up to him I left him but with a joy that he didn't have before.

Discipleship is where other people are. *Proverbs 3:6* "In all your ways acknowledge God and He will make your path straight." That means to Make Christ Known wherever you may be. When you are in public places you will see others. Maybe someone sitting all by himself who can be a prospect. Or a spiritual prompting to contact a friend. These people may turn out to be your contacts.

If you do not love to do this, confess your lack of love for God. God is in the changing business. I didn't even want to be a witness because I couldn't talk to people. But when God changed me, He became real. *Matthew 5:13-16* "You are the salt of the earth: but if the salt have lost his savor, wherewith shall it be salted? It is thenceforth good for nothing, but to be cast out, and to be trodden under foot of men. [14] You are the light of the world. A city that is set on a hill cannot be hid. [15] Neither do men light a candle, and put it under a bushel, but on a candlestick; and it gives light unto all that are in the house. [16] Let your light so shine before men..."

There are good leaders and bad leaders. One can know Scripture and still be disobedient. Good leaders make disciples. Where are they? Could the problem be secret sin? According to the following verses the problem was bad leadership. Jesus said they were hypocrites. They knew the law but they were disobedient to it.
Matthew 5:20 "For I say unto you, that except your righteousness shall exceed the righteousness of the scribes and Pharisees, you shall in no case enter into the kingdom of heaven."

CHAPTER 78 MOJAVE DESERT

Tony Heredia was a missionary to Colombia, South America, and I was a missionary to Ecuador. We were both home on furlough at the same time and one weekend we both went to the Mojave Desert to attend a missionary conference. There was nobody at the conference but what happened that day was an experience that I have shared many times for the last 45 years.

The conference was in the middle of the Mojave Desert in California. The church was located on a four corners, which was the whole town.

We waited for a while and since no one showed up we went to a nearby house to see if they knew anything. They didn't but as we were talking the man intrigued us and Tony and I were invited in. Here is the story the husband and his wife told us. It left us spellbound for the next several hours.

They had been Christians and for years. They went to church but that was the extent of their Christian life. They knew a little about the Bible, they didn't read the Bible together at home nor were they a witness to others because of their shy nature.

They told us that they did want to be active for the Lord but they didn't know how. They prayed together and told the Lord that they wanted to have God use them but because of their ignorance the Lord would have to show them how on a silver platter.

It wasn't too long after that when they were driving through the Mojave Desert they saw a teenage girl walking on the side of the road in the 120-degree heat. The girl was miles from the nearest house so they stopped the car to talk to her. She was dehydrated so they put her in the car and she fell asleep. When the couple brought the girl to their home they found out she had run away from home because of an argument, but now was humbled and wanted to be right with God. The couple wanted to help but they were helpless because of spiritual ignorance. The girl broke the silence by saying, "I overheard you in the car say that you go to church." They nodded their heads and then came a series of questions. "Tomorrow is Sunday, are you going to church? They said they were so the girl continued, "May I please go with you?" With that question everyone was spiritually inspired. God's love was manifested in a way that bonded them together. The couple insisted that she live with them.

The next day they were all sitting in a front pew thinking she would want to give her heart to the Lord. While the pastor was preaching the girl started to cry and the whole church gathered around her to pray for her. When the church heard her story and saw how humble she was, she immediately was accepted as one of them.

Each day at the house they read the Bible together and each gave their opinions and it was so much in agreement that they would study the Bible for hours and it became a daily habit.

The family's joy in the Bible was shared weekly in the church. It got to be that the center of attention was around that family. In every service the people wanted to hear what new was happening. It was amazing how this girl transformed the life of the whole church.

Then one day the girl said that she needed to go back to her folks and tell them what has happened to her. The couple refused to see her leave but after she pleaded with them they agreed but only under the condition that she would write them and visit them often.

The first letter came weeks later. She told them how her parents rejected the Bible and she felt so bad that she couldn't even write immediately. Now the church spent most of their services in prayer for the girl.

The next letter shared how her parents opened their hearts to the Lord and they started daily devotions. Then the next letter shared that their love for Jesus was made known to the neighbors. As the girl's letters were shared in the church it motivated the whole church to start making Christ known to others.

Then came a letter of great surprise. As people gathered together their house would not hold them all so they started building a church.

Tony and I were amazed how contagious God's love could be. The couple told us the story that had happened in just the few years since they found the girl on the roadside. Tony and I went back to the mission field but one day I would like to go back to the Mojave Desert and learn more about evangelism the right way. Today evangelism is treated as an unwelcome guest. Is it any wonder the church is deep into apostasy?

CHAPTER 79 EARLY CHURCH

We know little about the early church but one thing history agrees on is that each time a house meeting met together they had a public confession time. This kept the church pure. In Constantine's time the priests thought confession was taking up too much time in the church service so they confessed only to the priest at a private session. The Catholic Church still does this. Confession has a healing quality, both spiritually and physically. Confession should be done also to the person you sinned against. *James 5:16* "Confess your faults one to another, and pray one for another, that you may be healed. The effectual fervent prayer of a righteous man avails much."

Today there is little done in confessing sin, in the home and the church. Is it any wonder churches and homes are splitting up? The only way to clear the atmosphere is to confess you are wrong. *Matthew 6:13-15* "And lead us not into temptation, but deliver us from evil: For thine is the kingdom, and the power, and the glory, forever. Amen. [14] For if you forgive men their trespasses, your heavenly Father will also forgive you: [15] But if you forgive not men their trespasses, neither will your Father forgive your trespasses."

Jesus taught his disciples as He talked to the multitudes. His training was done by public evangelism. After the training, Jesus sent His disciples out to do what he taught them with the power to preach, heal, and cast out devils. The heart of Christ's teachings was all wrapped up in evangelism. Somehow or another we changed the system thinking that we have a better way. Today we only teach evangelism in the classroom.

Some Bible colleges have their students witness on their own but no one has shown discipleship to students by showing them. Jesus trained the twelve for three years but they still had doubts. I have had seven promises from the Bible for forty-five years, and I still have doubts whether they will come true in my lifetime on earth. But why don't I give up hope? It is because there are many more times I do not doubt. Satan finds times when we are vulnerable and the doubts come in, but during these times we must resist Satan and praise God.

CHAPTER 80 RESEARCH REPORT ON CHRISTIANS

The church has lost its ability to depart from evil. A report by a research organization reveals that based on 130 aspects of conduct and philosophy there is little difference between those who attend church and those who do not. The government makes civil laws and also enforces them, to keep order in the country. There is a great falling away from God these days because of disobedience to Scriptures. The sad thing is that this has been happening since 1957 and getting worse all the time. If our country doesn't have a revival soon—I can't think how I can complete that sentence.

CHAPTER 81 ENFORCING THE LAW AND SELF-DISCIPLINE

God makes spiritual laws but He doesn't force them on anyone. Neither does He allow Christians to force them on others. Church leaders must serve by showing the disciples by example. It is accomplished by self-discipline in obeying God's law under the

direction of the Holy Spirit. Christ's love had Judas grieve the Spirit within himself, and so he had nothing to live for. A person's unconfessed sin will take him out of circulation. When the church is pure, sin will be dealt with without any arguments. Read Chapter 54 on Judas.

Forcing a person to do what he should, without love, brings little effectiveness. Some years ago a nationwide discipleship program was started by telling others what to do through the ranks from the pastor on down, so everyone would be under a leader and he also would have someone under him.

A few years later that whole movement collapsed. That was not the way to have accountability and discipleship. Forcing Christians to do what is right doesn't work. We must have accountability to grow in love by holding one another in having self-discipline. Jesus had to have a Judas in the group to show the other eleven how important it is to have accountability.

Man can't organize the church to have unity. That is what denominations have done, thinking they are right but it only keeps them on their side of the fence.

CHAPTER 82 EFFECTIVENESS OF ARMED FORCES

When I was in basic training in the army I learned something that I can apply to the Christian life. The US Army is the most effective military army in the world, but it is only about 5 percent effective. I could hardly believe that. The reason for this is because when people are forced to take orders, without self-discipline, the efficiency rating is practically nothing. Self-discipline is part of the fruit of the Spirit for a good reason. Only parents can teach self-discipline by setting the example. Children want what they want, not what their parents want. God could so easily force people to obey but He chose to have us do it by self-discipline. It shows that God gives us the choice. There are different doctrines that men have made concerning free choice.

In the waiting room of a hospital today I met an electrical engineer. He shared what he did and I was impressed. I told him that I was a servant of Christ and for an hour and a half I was answering his questions, and he was impressed.

CHAPTER 83 IMPORTANT COMMANDS OF CHRIST

In the Gospels there are over fifty commands Jesus gives us. The most important one is love because all the other commands are based on love. You may keep your different doctrine but do not let it have priority over the commandments of Christ. Christianity should be based around what Jesus said and did.

It is obvious Satan is behind doctrine in order to cause disagreements. Doctrine is such a strong element in the Christian life that no denominational doctrine is willing to bend. Yesterday I met a lady in the waiting room of a hospital. We got into a conversation. She told me that her late husband was a Catholic and she is a Protestant. She said that no one was going to change her religion. God's love was not in their home. This couple's strong belief in their own church doctrine kept them from having prayer in their home.

Among the fundamental denominations, interpretations of doctrines have opposite meanings in some cases. I believe this is what Jesus calls the doctrine of man. It is hard for Christians to be in agreement with other Christians of different doctrines. This prevents genuine love. "They will know we are Christians by our love for one another." *John 13:34-35*

Doctrine doesn't make anyone great but Jesus says if you want to be the greatest be a servant of all.

John Calvin never met Martin Luther until one day when they were in the same city. They greeted each other with open arms but it wasn't long before they got into a heated discussion about doctrine. That lasted most of the day, with neither one giving an inch. The fellowship ended when they departed, only to see each other once again in their lifetime. Both were great men but that greatness didn't find love for each other.

The first five years of my Christian life I was indoctrinated so strongly that I couldn't even have Bible studies with other mainline denominations. I now have a Bible study with a strong Baptist and a strong Catholic. They love me because I do not speak against either of their doctrines. But I am not weak in doctrine. I use the teachings of Jesus as doctrine and neither side can refute.

CHAPTER 84 DISCIPLESHIP WITH YOUR CHILDREN

The dictionary says that the word "disciple" is a noun and the word "discipline" is a noun or a verb. This means that you can discipline a person but you can't disciple a person. This is true all through the New Testament—the word "disciple" is only used as a noun. Jesus has disciples. Jesus didn't disciple them nor did He discipline them. You would think Jesus would have disciplined Judas but He allowed Judas to continue to be the treasurer. That refers to the fact you can have disciples but you can't disciple them because to disciple them you are using the word as a verb. But the word discipline is a verb but Jesus didn't discipline them either. To use the word correctly you can teach a disciple but you can't disciple a disciple. Jesus taught his disciples to be followers of Him. Jesus said: Follow Me and I will make you fishers of men." Christ spent time with his disciples so that they would be like Him. Jesus was righteous and this is the way He wanted us to be. The closest we can come to be righteous is by confessing our sins. If we confess our sins Jesus cleanses us from all unrighteousness. *1 John 1:9.* But why didn't Jesus discipline them either? How did he discipleship his disciples. The goal of Jesus was to make his disciples to be like Himself by having the disciples live in righteousness.

Jesus became a servant to the point they obeyed everything He told them. To be a good leader you have to be servant of all. If a leader forces people to obey, he would be disciplining them and no one likes to be disciplined. The effective way to change others is to be a role model. Jesus did discipline Judas in love. But Judas loved money. Jesus told all of His disciples at the same time and He did this several times. He told them: "one of you will betray me." Each one of the disciples said, "Is it I?" This means we all have the potential to betray our authorities. This is why parents must spend time with their children practicing self-discipline themselves so their children will follow them as parents by practicing self-discipline also.

It is so easy to discipline your children which is difficult to do without getting upset, especially if they disobey over and over again. When you discipline in anger you may get their attention but why is it so detrimental? It is because your children will start to mimic you. The principal way to raise a child is to have yourself do everything you want them to do. In other words the parents must discipline themselves to teach self-discipline to their children. When parents argue with each other they are setting a bad example. A family must live in harmony. It is oneness that brings others in harmony. God is love. Jesus said in *John 17:22-23* "... be one with me as I am one with the Father that you may be one with each other." This is why it is important to love your enemy. It is an attempt to bring everyone together. Like drawing all men to Himself.

It is alright to discipline your children, but in love. As your children become older be willing to suffer with them. Jesus learned obedience by the things He suffered for our benefit. Righteousness is based on suffering. If you are not willing to suffer someone that has done you wrong, human nature will take over by the persuasion of temptation. Put the same restriction on yourself as you do on your children and they will take notice. Parents who yell at each other are setting a

bad example of love for their children. Parents' sins are handed down to their children, but so is righteousness handed down.

Parents need to watch their actions toward their children. Over 90 percent of abused children will abuse their children when they grow up. This goes for swearing, drinking, drugs, smoking, etc. Discipleship is showing others and getting to know them so that accountability can take place.

CHAPTER 85 DISCIPLESHIP WITH THE CHURCH

Just about every church that I have seen during my 50 trips through the States has had divisions. When the people can't resolve their differences in love, it leaves a scar that affects future growth in the church.

When I first became a Christian back in 1964 there was a big issue with divorce and remarriage. At that time there was a law in our civil government that it was illegal to get divorced and remarried. A law was then passed that it was legal to divorce under infidelity but to get remarried people were going to Mexico to marry, so finally the civil law accepted remarriage. The problem was that the church didn't want to change their Bible practices of divorce and remarriage and that is what created the problem. The church law and civil law having their differences. Christians involved would become angry, because divorce people had the law on their side. Soon after that time many of our national laws have come against Bible principles and to this day many have sued the church because the law was on their side. Slowly the church is changing to accept civil law as being the standard. Not only divorce and remarriage is accepted but so is abortion, and same sex marriages. The question is how does one love somebody that is in deep sin. If there is no love there will be anger and this is in my opinion the major cause of apostasy. Christians should not react to the laws of the land. We can make an appeal but never get angry. What would have happened if Jesus reacted to those who put Him on the cross? Many churches are being controlled by government law. Isn't it strange, in the beginning of our country the Christians in the government made biblical laws but now the laws are contrary to the Bible but only because Christians are not in politics any longer. Trying to change unbiblical laws would be reacting to sin. Our job is to change people. Today most churches do not have one new convert in a month. *Acts 16:5* "The church increased daily." The issue is causing Christians to leave the church at a fast rate. What do we do?

I believe that Daniel had a good solution. But he had to suffer much to remain true to Scriptures. Here is what he had to suffer: to see the enemy slaughter his own people, then be taken as a slave and made a eunuch. Daniel's choice to love his enemy the way God loved him. He ended up being the king's right hand man. Another example is Joseph was sold as a slave by his own brothers but he also remained pure in the sight of God and he became the second in command in the most powerful nation on the earth. You can love your enemy but it seems to be only one out of a million that can do this.

In modern times Martin Luther King Jr. chose to have freedom for his people by without retaliating and then die which he predicted will happen. All these people entered into a love that is not found in this world. Christians today can't even love one another. I believe that we must understand what real love is and cling to Jesus and not let go no matter what happens. Job said even if God would slay him, he would trust in Him. The highest standing in the Christian life is to be bless them that persecute us that we may be the children of our Father which is in heaven. *Matthew 5:12-13.*

If leaders practiced this in the church there would be no conflict. Jesus didn't have an open conflict with Judas. The Holy Spirit is a sensitive person but not offensive in any way. It is easy to grieve the Holy Spirit when we react. When one grieves the Holy Spirit he will also grieve his own spirit that God created in each one of us. It is our spirit that will bear witness with God's spirit that starts when one becomes a Christian and also matures as a Christian. When Judas grieved the Spirit of God, he also grieved the spirit God gave him. This may seem new to you. It was new to me also until I thought it all out.

CHAPTER 86 MEMORY OF ARMY LIFE

While I was in the US Army there was a sergeant who everyone spoke evil of. He would be so strict with rules and regulations that it kept him from liking anyone and no one liked him. I thought, how easy it was to talk about someone behind his or her back. I wasn't going to do that so I went to tell him this to his face and I almost got a court martial. When all the others heard what happened no one came to my rescue. But instead they told me how much trouble I was in. I can remember thinking, all I did was to tell him to his face what everyone else did behind his back.

If I went to our president and told him what Christians thought of him, would Christians back me up after my encounter at the White House? Jesus did not rebuke government leaders. When he was on trial for His life He never mentioned one thing wrong with the government. Jesus did give Pilate the hint when He told Pilate that the religious leaders committed the worse sin. It was spoken in love and after that time Pilate looked for a way to release Jesus.

The old nature tells us to complain but the new nature tells us to love. I didn't have love for the sergeant or for my friends that talked behind the sergeant's back. One must build himself up in the love of God before trying to be a hero. I was so upset with all my friends but I had to make a fast decision. There was only one thing to do. I went to the sergeant and told him I was sorry. Immediately the sergeant forgave me, but my friends never found out the truth of the matter.

I needed *Jude 1:20* "But ye, beloved, building up yourselves on your most holy faith, praying in the Holy Ghost ..."

Jesus would get into heavy discussions with the spiritual leaders. Jesus called them the children of the devil and they would tell Jesus that he was the prince of Beelzebub. Jesus rebuked his disciples several times and one time very strongly when he looked at Peter and said, "Satan, get behind me." But with Judas there was no hard rebuke but in the upper room when Jesus told the disciple that he would give the sop to the one who would betray him. All Jesus said, while giving Judas the sop was "Do what you have to do quickly." The bottom line is Jesus loved everyone so He was able to do things that we couldn't do unless we had the love of Jesus. We can lose our love even for our loved ones when we say things we ought not.

Many church splits today are because the person in sin will react when the rebuke was not done in love. It is not a question whether the person is right or wrong, but is the leader doing all that is possible to restore the one in sin, or does he just want justice? The person in sin will be able to sense love. Judas sensed love when he returned the thirty pieces of silver. He said that he betrayed innocent blood.

Years went by and you would think the mother and brothers and sisters of Jesus would see why He departed from them and entered into His ministry. But that wasn't the case. In *Mark 3* Mary had no idea that her Son, Jesus, had a ministry of preaching the gospel in public. In fact she thought He was going insane.

Mark 3:20-35 "and the multitude cometh together again, so that they could not so much as eat bread. [21] And when his friends heard *of it*, they went out to lay hold on him: for they said, He is beside himself. [22] And the scribes who came down from Jerusalem said, He hath Beelzebub, and by the prince of the devils casteth he out devils. [23] And he called them *unto him*, and said unto them in parables, how can Satan cast out Satan? [24]

And if a kingdom be divided against itself, that kingdom cannot stand. [25] And if a house be divided against itself, that house cannot stand. [26] And if Satan rise up against himself, and be divided, he cannot stand, but hath an end. [27] No man can enter into a strong man's house, and spoil his goods, except he will first bind the strong man; and then he will spoil his house. [28] Verily I say unto you, all sins shall be forgiven unto the sons of men, and blasphemies wherewith so ever they shall blaspheme: [29] But he that shall blaspheme against the Holy Ghost hath never forgiveness, but is in danger of eternal damnation: [30] Because they said, He hath an unclean spirit. [31] There came then his brethren and his mother, and, standing without, sent unto him, calling him. [32] And the multitude sat about him, and they said unto him, Behold, thy mother and thy brethren without seek for thee. [33] And he answered them, saying, who is my mother, or my brethren? [34] And he looked round about on them which sat about him, and said, Behold my mother and my brethren! [35] For whosoever shall do the will of God, the same is my brother, and my sister, and mother."

Today, the local church is doing little in training pastors, evangelists and missionaries. They believe someone else has to do the training, and even then it is mostly just classroom knowledge. The American church does not even know how to reproduce itself by starting other churches. Discipleship is virtually non-existent in the local church today. Churches that are growing are doing so by bringing in people from other churches. The Lord may be allowing divisions in the churches so they will open their eyes and come into a correct focus. The church is under heavy temptation today and has no understanding of what God expects. The seven churches of Revelation 2 and 3 should be a clue. Today we are living in the last of the seven churches, the age of apostasy.

2 Peter 2:9-11 [9]"The Lord knows how to deliver the godly out of temptations, and to reserve the unjust unto the Day of Judgment to be punished: [10] But chiefly them that walk after the flesh in the lust of uncleanness, and despise government. Presumptuous *are they*, self-willed, they are not afraid to speak evil of dignities. [11]Whereas angels, which are greater In power and might, bring not railing accusation against them before the Lord."

Acts 2:30 through Acts 2:46 "Therefore being a prophet, and knowing that God had sworn with an oath to him, that of the fruit of his loins, according to the flesh, he would raise up Christ to sit on his throne; [31] He seeing this before spoke of the resurrection of Christ, that his soul was not left in hell, neither his flesh did see corruption. [32] This Jesus hath God raised up, whereof we all are witnesses. [33] Therefore being by the right hand of God exalted, and having received of the Father the promise of the Holy Ghost, he hath shed forth this, which you now see and hear. [34] For David is not ascended into the heavens: but he said himself, The LORD said unto my Lord, Sit thou on my right hand, [35] Until I make thy foes thy footstool. [36] Therefore let all the house of Israel know assuredly, that God hath made that same Jesus, whom you have crucified, both Lord and Christ. [37] Now when they heard *this*, they were pricked in their heart, and said unto Peter and to the rest of the apostles, Men *and* brethren, what shall we do? [38] Then Peter said unto them, Repent, and be baptized every one of you in the name of Jesus Christ for the remission of sins, and you shall receive the gift of the Holy Ghost. [39] For the promise is unto you, and to your children, and to all that are afar off, *even* as many as the Lord our God shall call. [40] And with many other words did he testify and exhort, saying, Save yourselves from this untoward generation. [41] Then they that gladly received his word were baptized: and the same day there were added *unto them* about three thousand souls.

[42] And they continued steadfastly in the apostles' doctrine and fellowship, and in breaking of bread, and in prayers. [43] And fear came upon every soul: and many wonders and signs were done by the apostles. [44] And all that believed were together, and had all things common; [45] And sold their possessions and goods, and parted them to all *men*, as every man had need. [46] And they, continuing daily with one accord in the temple, and breaking bread from house to house, did eat their meat with gladness and singleness of heart ..."

We fight our government and think we are doing our job but the Great Commission is idle. We are the only country that permits Christianity in which the Christian faith is not growing in numbers. The church should be ashamed of itself. Not even the angels could speak against civil government and yet the people take the side of the political party that they are in favor of, which makes them presumptuous, thinking the other side is evil. What this does is to eliminate people's spiritual concern for them.

President Washington never wanted a political party system in the country for he knew what it would do. But a party system did start and this is the way it happened: Thomas Jefferson and Alexander Hamilton were two brilliant men who had opposite understanding on how our government should function. When no one was able to settle their disagreements, the party system began. It all started by the disagreements of these two men.

Everyone knows today that Congress is a major problem in our country and seemingly it will continue being a problem because the Republicans and the Democrats have contrary ideas on how to run our country in almost everything.

The same is true in the church today. Because brilliant men in the faith have interpreted the Bible in many different ways that cannot be resolved, the spiritual party system called denominationalism began. It took me over forty-five years as a Christian to see how that was wrong in my own life and there was a necessity for a change.

This change came about when I started to stress the two things of the greatest importance in Christianity. These two things are so important that they will have lasting effects even after this world will be burned up. They are: first the Word of God which is the same yesterday, today, and forever. And the second is the souls of people. Everyone who was born on this earth will have eternity. But by far the majority will have eternal suffering.

Matthew 7:13-14 "Enter you in at the strait gate: for wide is the gate, and broad is the way, that leads to destruction, and many there be which go in thereat: [14] Because strait is the gate, and narrow is the way, which leads unto life, and few there be that find it."

There are many Scriptures that tell us that loving our enemies is where the power is and Jesus proved it with His death. It was His love for those that killed Him for two reasons; The first reason was Jesus didn't react and the second reason is that He forgave His enemies and said it while suffering on the cross just before He died. Church discipline today is based on who is right, not who is willing to suffer for being right. *1 Peter 2:19-25.* When conflict comes neither side is willing to suffer because they feel so justified.

The Christian life is focused on the death and the resurrection of Jesus Christ. It is not understandable in human standards so we need to meditate on the Word of God to know the Truth. Jesus uses his own death and resurrection to explain everything that happens in our life on a daily basis. If we humble ourselves when suffering comes, a joy of resurrection will follow. Death represents suffering. And if we suffer with Christ we will reign with Him. Dying to our own reasoning when we think we are right is difficult. Abraham had to die to his own reasoning when the Lord told him to kill his son. God told Abraham that he would be the father of many nations and the qualification was to suffer when he was told to kill his own son. How unreasonable can that be?

Abraham obeyed God's command to kill his son, although it seemed totally unreasonable to him. It wasn't until the very last second that an angel held back Abraham's hand. At that last moment his

suffering was at its peak. We accept this story because it is now history and we understand, but when a similar situation happens in our lives we complain.

I see this many times as a witness. A man I met today wanted God but didn't want to talk about God. I dropped the subject, gave him a compliment and said goodbye. I left on a friendly basis. Later I thought, what it would take to have that man understand that public ministry is what Christianity is all about.

Abraham had to believe what God said, beyond his own reasoning. This made Abraham a type of Christ when he was willing to put his son on the altar. By this act of faith Abraham became the father of many nations. If God takes away your baby, you may not understand it and you may hold it against God but what the Lord wants is to put the power of the resurrection of Christ in you by trusting in Him.

Every time we complain there is a resistance to God's purpose in our life. It means we have failed the test. God's ways are higher than our ways. This is all hinged on being willing to suffer for Christ's sake. Suffering should be major doctrine and it is also a commandment of Christ and if we suffer with Christ we will reign with Him. If we are going to have to suffer with or without Christ, what is more logical?

2 Corinthians 1:5-7 [5] "For as the sufferings of Christ abound in us, so our consolation also abounds by Christ. [6] And whether we be afflicted, *it is* for your consolation and salvation, which is effectual in the enduring of the same sufferings which we also suffer: or whether we be comforted, *it is* for your consolation and salvation. [7] And our hope of you *is* steadfast, knowing, that as you are partakers of the sufferings, so *shall you be* also of the consolation."

Philippians 3:10 "That I may know him, and the power of his resurrection, and the fellowship of his sufferings, being made conformable unto his death ..."

Colossians 1:24 "Who now rejoice in my sufferings for you, and fill up that which is behind of the afflictions of Christ in my flesh for his body's sake, which is the church ..."

Hebrews 2:10 "For it became him, for whom *are* all things, and by whom *are* all things, in bringing many sons unto glory, to make the captain of their salvation perfect through sufferings."

1 Peter 2:19-25 [19] "For this *is* thankworthy, if a man for conscience toward God endure grief, suffering wrongfully. [20] For what glory *is it*, if, when you be buffeted for your faults, you shall take it patiently? But if, when you do well, and suffer *for it*, you take it patiently, this *is* acceptable with God. [21] For even hereunto were you called: because Christ also suffered for us, leaving us an example, that you should follow his steps: [22] Who did no sin, neither was guile found in his mouth: [23] Who, when he was reviled, reviled not again; when he suffered, he threatened not; but committed *himself* to him that judgeth righteously: [24] Who his own self bare our sins in his own body on the tree, that we, being dead to sins, should live unto righteousness: by whose stripes you were healed. [25] For you were as sheep going astray; but are now returned unto the Shepherd and Bishop of your souls."

CHAPTER 87 US LOVING GOD IS A FAR CRY FROM GOD LOVING US

The love of the world has made so much of an impact on us humans that we have no idea what God's love is all about.

First John 4:10 "In this is love, not that we love God, but that He loved us." I believe that the closer we understand how much God loved us; we will be able to love others more. The love in marriage brings two people together but the love of God is capable in bringing the entire world together. The love of the world has made so much of an impact of us humans that we have no idea what we are missing. But the people of the world not only don't understand but they persecute Christians that do have understanding. And if Christians had a better understanding of

God's love they would have a greater desire to tell others and on a daily basis. But neither do married couples believe the power of God's love. After they get married many times they allow conflicts to become stronger than forgiveness. According to 1 John 1:9 every time we forgive we become righteous.

I thought lust was one of the strongest forces that exist in this world and I was right. Lust is from the god of this world and he deceived me to believe that he is God. God's love is genuine. Satan's love is lust. Lust has a drawing power that comes from evil. God has a drawing power in Christ, "If I be risen from the dead, I will draw all men unto Me." The righteousness of God starts with the death of Christ.

This evening I stopped at a restaurant to get a sandwich. I asked the waitress if she was going to heaven; she said that she always tries to be righteous. I said that is fine but God says that the righteousness of man is as filthy rags with God, so I think you need a little help. She agreed but walked away indicating she didn't want to know where that help would come from.

1 John 4:12 "No man has seen God at any time. The love of the world has made so much of an impact on us humans that we have no idea what God's love can do. God's love is beyond my ability to think." *Ephesians 3:19.* "If we love one another, God dwells in us, and His love is perfected in us." *1 John 2:5.* Through this Scripture and Matthew 5:48 we can have perfection in love. Love being the greatest of all the commandments of Jesus should be something we should strive for. I believe that the church has fallen short of this so much that it is bringing us into apostasy at a fast rate. To love God with a pure love is what we need and to love everyone we know. God so loved the world. (God loves everyone He knows.)

As soon as we get into a disagreement and we conclude the other person is absolutely wrong, we subconsciously think we are absolutely right. The reason Satan tempts this way goes right back to why he was cast out of heaven. He wanted to be equal with God. Satan gets his power in the tree of knowledge of good and evil. We should never study what is evil. Negative and evil thoughts are what Satan wants us to dwell on. The devil wants us to think about the knowledge of good and evil, to come up with the solution of all our problems.

God wants us to concentrate on light, which is righteousness, and to be simple discern what is evil. *Roman 16:18-19.* The word simple here means "not knowing much." "God is light and in Him is no darkness at all."

Satan is darkness but his domain goes right into the knowledge of light. "Satan appears as an angel of light." *2 Corinthians 11:14.* This is the way Satan traps us. If we had all the knowledge from one extreme of Evil to the other extreme of Good, we would be able to resolve any problem. God doesn't want us to go out of the light from where He abides. Any negative thought or shade of gray will make us more like Satan. Thinking of anything bad that has happened to us will only induce worry. This is why praise is so important. Trying to eliminate the problem by our self brings worry and frustration.

There is a song that goes something like this: "Praise Him in the morning, praise Him at noon time and praise Him when the sun goes down. Praise Him all the time." We should think on the how great God is. This is called meditation.

Genesis 2:8-9 "Now the Lord God had planted a garden in the East of Eden, and there He put the man that He had formed. *Verse 9* ... and the Lord made all kinds of trees grow out of the ground. Trees that were pleasing to the eye and good for food. In the middle of the garden were the tree of life and the tree of knowledge of good and evil."

The tree of life is Jesus and the tree of knowledge of good and evil is where Satan gets his power. But remember it was God that planted both trees. Satan became the god of this world through the tree of knowledge of good and evil that God planted. God gave the power of temptation to Satan. What he couldn't have in heaven he tries to have us to believe on the earth.

The earth was made for humans. But since Adam and Eve failed they still had to rely on the resources on the earth to sustain life, so Satan is not gaining anything for himself, but from what he knows he tempts humans to fail the Grace of God. So the only pleasure he gets out of his tempting humans is to have us be punished with him in the lake of fire. The devil comes to kill, steal, and to destroy and he does it by deceiving.

We must remember that God is always in control. God allowed Satan to kill Jesus. It is connected to the same reasoning why God allows Satan to tempt us. Jesus learned obedience by the things He suffered and we do also, through the tree of knowledge of good and evil Satan continues to rebel against God. But not for himself any longer because he has been defeated. Misery wants company. Satan was a liar from the beginning and he comes to kill, steal, and destroy. He doesn't win us over by what he is but by what he wanted to be. He wanted to be like God. God wants us to be like Jesus.

Satan knows more about God than the best of us. So, his temptation is a mixture of good and evil. People do not want evil unless they have entered into a reprobate mind in which they think Good is evil and Evil is good. The Bible says that God is light and in Him is no darkness at all. God doesn't leave his domain of light but Satan leaves his domain of darkness and becomes as an angel of light to deceive us. *2 Cor. 11:14* "And no wonder for Satan himself transforms himself into an angel of light." We are in this world but not of this world. This is why we need to live only for what stands for light, which is truth and righteousness. This is why our life has to be centered on the Bible. Reading the Bible doesn't make us like Christ but the application of the Bible does. That means obedience to the Holy Spirit.

Our lifetime here on earth must consist of being more like Jesus and showing discipleship to others to do the same. Getting into any worldly activity to persuade others to accept Christ will be insignificant. Christians need to be filled with Christ so that others will see the light and come into salvation. So how does Satan tempt us to be equal with God? Let's go back to Genesis concerning the conversation he had with Eve:

Genesis 3:1-6 "Now the serpent was more cunning than any beast of the field which the Lord God had made. And he said to the woman, has God indeed said, you shall not eat of every tree of the garden." Verse 2 "And the woman said to the serpent, we may eat the fruit of the trees of the garden," Verse 3 "But of the fruit of the tree which is in the midst of the garden, God has said, you shall not eat it nor shall you touch it, lest you die." Verse 4 "And the serpent said to the woman, you will not surely die." Verse 5 "For God knows that in the day you eat of it your eyes shall be open and you will be like God, knowing good and evil." Verse 6 "So when the woman saw that the tree was good for food, that it was pleasant to the eyes, and a tree desirable to make one wise, she took of its fruit and ate. She also gave to her husband with her, and he ate."

Notice in Genesis 3:1-6 that Satan mixes God's truth with the devil's lies to deceive us.

Eve believed that eating the fruit would give her understanding of what was right and wrong. But the thought that she would be equal to God didn't occur to her. She was deceived and ate the fruit and gave it to her husband. He was with her and heard the whole conversation so he was deceived also when he ate.

In my youth I fell into temptations that formed strong habits which followed me into my Christian life, both in lust and pride. When we think the other person is wrong automatically it makes us right. So that makes us equal with God. I have an understanding of this now but I was deceived for years.

As I was sharing this with another person he completely agreed with me. I told him that was beautiful that he understands

this so easily. I said, "That makes you the better man."

But as we continued to talk he told me of a problem he had in the past and I detected un-forgiveness in his attitude so I asked him, "Did you forgive that person?" He was speechless. It showed me that we are all alike. When we are not thinking of an offense involving us, we can know how wrong offenses and unforgiving are, but on the other side of the fence, when we face an offense, in real life, our justification puts us into a mode of un-forgiveness.

We may want to be innocent because we are right. The problem is when our attitude is not right we have sinned also. Just the thought of anger can be like committing murder.

The only way sin is handed down from one person to another is because of the other person's sin. His sin will cause you to sin and without a Savior there is no hope. Jesus died for all sin. This means that we do not love the person we are talking to. We must separate the person from his sin or we will hate the person and his sin together.

A non-believer may want to be innocent but if somebody robs you it can make you become angry. It is easy to see that the person who robbed us has sinned but if we do not look upon our reaction as sin we will be angry, then bitter and after that can come revenge.

According to Matthew 5:22 you can be guilty of murder. So now that makes your sin greater than the sin of the robber. In my travels through the States I have seen many Church divisions. Each side thinks the other side is the one in the wrong. In many cases both sides have wrong attitudes. And when both sides justify their anger, it will turn to bitterness. Until there is humility both sides are in sin and it can go on for years. Until this sin is dealt with, the church will be no better than the person in sin even though he may be only one person out of many in the church. When Akan's sinned in the Old Testament, all the people suffered for it and they lost their battles with enemies until the sin was dealt with.

Several times I heard of church problems being taken to court and the guilty party would win. Laws are not on the side of the Bible any longer.

Jesus never argued with Judas. The first thing we do when we disagree is to argue. Jesus resolved the sin of Judas by love. Jesus loved Judas unto the end.

God's pure love will never fail, the Bible says. Judas tried to respond to that love by saying he had betrayed innocent blood but his sin was so much a part of him that he grieved the Holy Spirit and had no desire to live. That was the unpardonable sin.

A pastor told me that "Joe" was a member of long standing in his church, but he became critical of the pastor's preaching and during the service Joe looked at the wall with a negative expression. This irritated the pastor. Then the pastor said that he needed to be honest with me, that he didn't like Joe. I did see he was being honest but that wasn't being truthful. The truth is to love your enemy. That pastor could not see where his lack of love was wrong. He wanted to get rid of Joe, not help him. They may not call it hate or anger but you can see it in a person's attitude. There is no way that pastor would be able to help Joe until he confessed his sin of anger or lack of love.

Stories like this have happened in churches over and over again. God keeps on having mercy but there is a last time for mercy that is the unpardonable sin. Mercy is God giving us another chance. Grace is having us come out of our sin. That is why grace is necessary for salvation and growth in Christ.

I have traveled through the States over fifty times and I have seen this hundreds of times. I can only remember two times that I was about to help and both times I stumbled into resolving the problem without knowing exactly how I did it. Now I have an understanding. I have also learned that if both sides are not willing to forgive, no one can help resolve the conflict. If only one side is willing to forgive, that party must pray for love and when God gives it to him, he must re-approach the other party. God will give you love for your enemy but you must be determined to want it.

We may not be able to see things clearly and know how to help church splits until we build up our love to a new level. There is no way that pastor would be able to help Joe until he confessed his sin of anger or lack of love. It took me years before I understood that spiritual principle but it was really quite simple. Usually, church problems are solved by wisdom not knowledge. With our love for God we will see the other person's sin clearly, but it is true the other way around also. So we need each other.

To clarify accountability, it is two people giving permission to tell each other when the other is wrong. But it will never work just with the permission without God's pure love. Even with accountability we need to know when to back off. All arguments hinge on what is right and wrong. As we argue and debate, our love can't be found. Forgiveness is God's way of giving us righteousness.

1 John 1:9 "God will forgive and cleanse us from all unrighteousness." And if we forgive our enemies we will be cleansed from unrighteousness and will be able to help the sinner. Satan will tempt us to have conflicts. It goes for any two people or any two nations. In all cases it can mean war. As much as I see my problem, I know I will still have trouble with this in the future. I need accountability.

If our thoughts become negative, we are in trouble because Satan is in control. We should not learn about evil. See Romans 16:19. Also Philippians 4:8 It only brings negative thoughts. With God's love we will be able to discern evil. When we are right with God, we will have the ability to see evil when it comes.

Our country is depending on education to develop our nation. Education without God will make us wanting to be as God.

Knowledge can replace God and it is increasing continuously. Heavy study taxes the mind. At a university I was talking to a girl who was taking an overloaded schedule and also planning on taking summer courses. I asked her why she was rushing her education so much. She said, "Only for one reason. I want to be able to go on living again as soon as possible."

I told her to try living for the Lord. That didn't seem to make much sense to her. Suicide among college students is the number one cause of death among teenagers. Education has corrupted religion even for the Christian. Classroom study is not discipleship like Jesus showed us in the Bible. On the job training has always been the best way to learn. In this way knowledge and virtue will strengthen each other. Knowledge without virtue will be argumentative. "Knowledge puffs a person up and love edifies."

Jesus said, "By taking thought no man can add one cubit to his statue." *Matthew 6:27* Just before that verse it says: "take no thought what you should eat or drink ..." What this is talking about is worry. The more we trust in Jesus the less we have to worry. Memorizing Scriptures is so important. Many tell me they can't memorize. They say it takes too much time. That is why I tell them to memorize; it is a way to spend more time with Jesus. If you have to repeat Scripture twenty times and still do not memorize it, you have succeeded in having spent more time with the Lord. The real reason why we do not want to memorize is because it is hard work.

The Christian life is trying to please God at all times. Pray without ceasing, and in everything we do, we should do all for the glory of God. In marriage with children this will be difficult because of all the family obligations. That is why it is mandatory to plan a time for the whole family once a day so the spirit of God will be present. God longs for a "time out" with Him.

Hate is the opposite of love. It is one or the other. Every time I confess my hate for someone I must spend time on a verse that tells me to love. Then every time hate comes into my mind I can replace it with the love scripture. It may take some time before I love the person I hated, but when the transformation does take place, it is immediate. It will hit you suddenly even though it took you a long time to get there. The presence of God will be so real that you will feel unworthy to be in His presence. That tells me that there is no gradual change. In fact the change is so fast that you believe it is a miracle. When Jesus appeared to Peter he had a feeling of unworthiness. Peter said, "Lord depart from me, a sinner, I am unworthy."

Any unresolved conflict makes us like the living dead. It is like being in prison and Jesus says we will not come out until we have paid the price. That means trust in Jesus who paid the price. We must analyze our thoughts according to the Word of God to have application. At salvation we must confess our own sin to get right with God. When in an argument we must confess our own sin before we can help the person in his sin. We must see that an argumentative attitude makes us a sinner. Two people in sin can't help each other and it doesn't matter who is right. It is a matter of sin not terminology or theology. We are smart enough to see what is right and wrong, but not wise enough to see sin. Many times smart people are more apt to be deceived.

Confession is necessary at salvation but just as necessary every time we sin after salvation. After confessing sin we become righteous again. So salvation only gets us started. I find myself confessing to God almost every day. Until I started analyzing my life in God's presence, I thought I was pretty good.

We need to be righteous at least once a day. That way we can grow in Christ daily. The opposite is true. Sin grows also. Sin doesn't stay on the same level. The wages of sin is more sin. Being upset can turn into anger and then bitterness. Satan wants us to be so filled with condemnation that we will destroy ourselves like Judas did. In *Matthew 5:23-26* Jesus doesn't even want us to pray when there is any conflict toward another, however small the conflict may seem to be. First be reconciled with your brother and then you can return to prayer.

People have asked me how they can confess the sin when the other person is wrong. What happens is that the other person's sin becomes our sin if we get upset. If we do not love the sinner, the sinner's sin becomes our sin. *Matthew 7:1-5* tells us this. If we react to someone that is in sin then we are more wrong than he is. Why? Because we are to help people see their sin and not make it worse.

The sin of anger is like killing someone. (*Matthew 5:22*) When Jesus was talking to Pilate, Jesus said the ones who handed me over to you have committed the greater sin. Why did Jesus say that, when Pilate was the one who put Jesus on the cross? It is because the mob did it in anger, so they were guilty of murder. So even though Pilate ordered to have Jesus crucified the blood was on the hands of the angry mob.

I have heard people confessing this way: "Yes I was wrong but you were wrong also." That may be true but it doesn't hold water. One can't confess his sin at the same time he is confessing the sin of the other person. First cast the beam out of your own eye. One sin is not greater than another and you can't confess the sins of the other unless you have love. That is how Jesus took upon himself the sins of the world.

Daniel in *Daniel 9:20* was able to confess the sins of the people after he confessed his own sins. This is why accountability is so important. We can't see our sin at the same time we are seeing the sins of another. We conclude that if the other person is wrong, I must be right. This is why others can see our sins before we can see them. And what that says is that we need accountability. I see that this is what is missing in all the churches that have had a division.

CHAPTER 88 FORMING A NEW HABIT

In the last several chapters there are some repeats. I thought the repeats are important to be mentioned again but I have also added some new insights.

In the New Testament there are several lists of sin. The lists are found in *Galatians 5*, *Colossians 3*, and *Romans 1*. We find a good summary of these sins in *1 John 2:16*. "All that is of the world is the lust of the flesh, the lust of the eyes and the pride of life." This sums up sin in three categories: 1. Immorality, 2. Materialism, 3. Pride.

Almost every time a man stares at a beautiful woman he thinks of lust. Yet he wants to marry for love. But after marriage there is still a temptation to look at other women. How does a man overcome lustful desires for a woman? Jesus says that whosoever looks at a woman to lust after her has already committed adultery.

This is a hard saying for a man to follow. In national news I heard that a man thinks of sex every seventy seconds. Even the best of men have committed adultery and who knows how many times. Does this mean that the commandments of Christ are impossible to keep? Or maybe we should just try the best we can and think that is sufficient?

Lust and love are closely related, but love is giving to the needs of others and lust is satisfying one's own fleshly desires. There is another way of looking at what seems to be impossible. The Bible says what is impossible with men is possible with God. So we can rule out the impossibility, but how? It is habits that cause a person to repeat sin. We need to break these habits but how do we do it? Satan counterattacks the commands of Christ with a temptation of the flesh, the knowledge of which we can use to form a good habit. A good habit can't just substitute a bad habit— but God has a way. The Bible says love not the world nor the things of the world. He that loves the world, the love of God is not in him.

This should give us the clue that God's love is stronger than any other form of lust. But we can have pseudo presentation forms of love to remind us of God's love and hence turn temptation to a victory. First, confess being upset, angry, or bitter as sin and ask the Lord to put His love in the place of the pseudo love. God will remind us of sin so we will be able to cast it out. If we try to reason it out, it will only give us worry. You may have to do this many times before victory comes. For example when lust comes to your mind confess it as sin and substitute that lust for God's pure love. Satan wants to torment us with his temptations, but now God is having Satan's devices to help us to transfer our thinking onto His Word. As we put this in practice daily it will form a divine habit. The joy of this new habit will overcome the joy you had in the flesh. This will prove to us that God is more powerful than Satan. Society says that a habit can be formed in about forty days. This means that the transfer will take time, but once the power of God's Word takes over, the bondage will leave. That is victory in Jesus.

We all want miracles in forming new habits and God in His mercy will break some old habits immediately to show His power. To break other habits is a challenge. We all want to be great in something in this world although we know it will take much hard work to achieve this. It takes special abilities to be great in sports or to be the president of a company but God has no respecter of persons to achieve something spiritually. The challenge is for men and women, young and old, ignorant and the wise. This shows us how great God is and is worthy of praise.

Satan is the god of the world and there are many bad habits connected in all the activities the world has. God wants us to be challenged in creating Biblical habits to be more like Jesus and what a joy is to have fellowship with Jesus inside of us. This is how God's grace changes us. Grace takes us from the joy of the world to the joy of being used of God. God's grace is not anything we have done within ourselves, yet we have our part in

self-discipline so the transaction will take place.

Again let us review. The first requirement is to picture the old habit as sin and confess it to God as sin. We must confess the sin as many times as needed. There is no limit. Satan will not give up without a struggle so we need persistence. When Peter wanted to know how many times we need to forgive others, Jesus said seventy times seven. Satan will repeat the thought of the sin but every time the temptation comes we spring our thoughts to God's love, which is stronger, but there is a suffering we go through. As we cast down Satan's temptation, a war goes on in our mind between two spiritual forces. This is what causes the sufferings. When we can't bear it any longer, the angels will minister to us like they did to Jesus after He was tempted. I can't explain it any better than that. One has to experience it for himself. Once we see the Grace of God at work the suffering is worth it all.

When you confess God's love your feelings will not change immediately, but they will change after a number of times of being tempted. The Lord will put your mind at peace. Temptation will be replaced with God's love. It takes endurance but grace will have us succeed. See *2 Peter 1:5-7*. We add to our faith, virtue, knowledge, tolerance, patience, godliness, brotherly kindness, to love. These are the steps of endurance to reach love.

This may not seem to work because you still have lust. I used to think that as good habits increase little by little, the habit of lust will decrease little by little. This seemed logical to me but when I put this in action I found that God does something we can't expect to happen in our human nature.

When I use the springboard affect to form a new habit I find that God is faithful to remind me to cast out the old habit and put in the new habit. This will continue over a period of time, but here is the miracle. After a struggle for a while, all of sudden you will sense God has taken over and replaced lust with His love. This is immediately. When this happens you know you have made contact with God because He changed your way of thinking immediately—but only after a great struggle. This is not humanly possible. This is a challenge that will make you know that Jesus is living inside of you and is stronger than Satan. The challenge is striving for God's power and not letting your feelings make you give in. In the past I was able in my own strength to have the struggle continue over long periods of time and many times I would fall right back into the temptation. I lacked expectation. I needed to expect God to do what He said He would do.

Chapter 89 OBEDIENCE

Jesus is God but also human like us, yet none of Christ's love was for the things of this world. Jesus lived on the bare essentials. He didn't have a house to live in nor did he have money for personal pleasures. Neither did he have any rights. Jesus also had to fight off temptation the same way we do.

Matthew 4:3-4 "Jesus was tempted to turned stones into bread. Jesus said to take no thought for our own life. To have something for our own benefit is tempting God." *James 1:13* "let no man say when he is tempted, "I am being tempted by God," to blame God for cancer, or for killing your child. Tempting God means to blame God for what He allows in your life.

:6-7 Jesus was tempted to use his power to jump off a building and not get hurt. That would be suicide for us. When the thought of suicide comes, God gives us the ability to immediately cast it down as temptation. The same for any discouragement like boredom, frustration, and so on. We can turn temptations into the power of God after we have suffered for a while. Jesus suffered so much in temptation that angels had to come and minister to him. *Matthew 4:11*

In Matthew 4:8-10 Jesus was tempted with all the pleasures of the world. We can be tempted by complaining about not having things we think we need, which is just a small,

small part of the world. Sometimes humans are even willing to die for what we think we have a right to.

God put all these temptations on Christ and we will be tempted in the same way. But the temptations on Jesus were at full strength. God doesn't give us more than what we can handle. It is up to us to accept the intensity in which we are tempted. The more we can bear the more mature we will be. We need to be strong in the Lord.

We do not like the suffering. But without Christ, think of eternal suffering in the lake of fire, torment day after day forever and ever. The little suffering on this earth is but a drop in the bucket, Paul says, in comparison to eternal glory.

The first temptation is wanting a miracle, thinking God owes us something. Many times I hear people blame God for innocent babies dying. God has grace for all this and He wants to give us grace in every temptation Satan gives us. We are now living in the dispensation of grace and how many times do we resist it. It happens every time we complain or have any negative thought.

The second temptation is to think we can take foolish risks. Or if we get hurt and sick, to blame it on God. It seems like many of our prayers go unanswered, which will hinder our faith if we complain. We must believe that God is righteous and loves us starting on the inside. "Know you not that the kingdom of God is within you." Job was willing to have God slay him but still trust in Him. He knew that God had control for not only his life but also everything in this universe.

This is why worship and praise is so important. Heaven is full of praise and all the time. In heaven Jesus will be our life support at all times with no temptation forever. God Himself shall wipe all tears from our eyes. That means no more pain or suffering.

And the third temptation is wanting what the world has to offer. All that is of the world is lust, riches and pride. Resisting the devil is not easy because that would be denying ourselves of the things the flesh wants. Satan has a counterpart for every good thing God has for us. We as humans get upset when Satan's counterpart comes. But all we need to do is to replace this counterpart with the real thing God has for us. For example: Satan will have things happen to bring hate into our thoughts and if we complain we are shut off from what God wants for us. But if we understand that God's love is much greater than hate we can have victory. In most cases the victory will not be immediate, we must believe it by faith until the feeling of victory comes. All we need to do is to find a verse on love and have that verse override the hate Satan gave us. An example is *Ephesians 3:19*. It will seem like bondage for a while but when the victory comes it will be all of a sudden. And that is what we call a miracle. Miracles without the suffering will make us proud. The multitudes followed Jesus because of the miracles, but because of their pride Jesus told them many times to not tell anyone of their healing. They should have been preaching the kingdom of God is at hand.

Few of the multitude became disciples. At one time Jesus had seventy disciples but they all left Him because His sayings were too hard to take. See *John chapter six*.

We want to have our cake and to eat it too. We want God but we want to satisfy the flesh also. God's ways are higher than our ways. We do have to suffer in the flesh to see it. *1 Peter 4:1* ... suffering in the flesh controls sin.

It is important to spend time in the Word daily and to confess our sins. We need to change our joy from the flesh to the spirit. The spirit is willing but the flesh is weak. So the first thing to do when evil comes is to confess that you were wrong to meditate on it. After that, search for a Scripture on love to replace the hate. Then sit on this Scripture until you will find out that God has more power than Satan. If we continue to think about the hate, worry will conquer you. If you meditate on the promise, God will bless you, after you have suffered for a while. Nobody in

his or her right mind would think God wants us to suffer. The suffering comes from the god of this world. We, passing through this world, will have to suffer as Christ did when He came to this world.

Remember God is in control. The baby Jesus was very close to being killed. The timing pointer in your car is very close to the rotating flywheel but no closer. If we do not thank God for suffering we will not reign with Christ. Our joy is to come from the things of God and not of the world. If we are not forming new habits the old ones will still be our desires. We need to believe that God's Word can be applied to our life.

God is love and this love can do what is impossible for us humans. We can love our enemy but it is only possible with God. Yet almost every church in America has had splits and divisions because they can't understand the Father's love. When our enemy comes against us, we can't be innocent because human nature is to react. When we react we have sinned against God. This is why it is so important to love our enemy. If we react long enough we have anger and bitterness and with these negative attitudes we cannot love our enemy.

Any hate toward others puts Satan in control and he will stay in control until we confess our sin. If we can't love, we can't help others. God loved us while we were still sinners. It isn't easy to understand this until we plead for God's love. With bad habits Satan is in control more than we think. We just do not want to give up our negative attitude because we all want to judge the other person's sin and not our own sin. That is what happens when our emotions get stirred up. Satan controls our mind. Others can see we are wrong but we don't want to listen to them. Now the person that wants to help us will become our enemy.

We first want God to deal with the sin of our enemy and not our own sin. That is not the way God operates. *Matthew 7:1-5* We must first be willing to confess our sin. This is an important aspect of grace. God gives grace to the humble. Jesus had to die in the hands of His enemies before He had control over sin. That includes our sins because it was our sins that put Him on the cross. It was over 2,000 years ago, but Christ is the same yesterday, today, and forever. It was like it happened today. The amazing thing about it is that Jesus is able to die for people who haven't been born yet because the past, present and the future is time. There is no time with God. This was all planned out before the foundations of the world.

Humility is necessary for grace. So if you are reacting in anger you have fallen into temptation. God allows the temptation to test us. But reacting to our enemy is failing the test and falling into temptation. We need others to help us but pride will resist that help.

The Old Testament had laws and Jesus did not come to destroy the law but to fulfill the law. The law of the New Testament changes the laws of the Old Testament. And it is a law of the Old Testament that says to kill your enemy, but Christ's law says to love your enemy. That law Jesus talks about is His commandments. Somehow we think our doctrines are more important than Christ's command to love. In Matthew 22:40 Jesus says that all truth is summed with His Love. We can see disobedience easily in our children, but our children can't see it because they are just doing what they want to do. Parents are children of God and they have the same struggle in disobedience. Sin is passed down.

Obedience is important in many aspects of life. We must be obedient to the laws of our country, to our employer, our teachers, and children must obey their parents. Obedience brings harmony and unity. Obedience to civil law will eliminate crime. But without love there can't be obedience that would be lasting. Obedience to our authority on this earth is what God expects for us to be obedient to Him.

The problem is that we don't have the fear of God when obeying human authority. We see other humans as sinners like ourselves and we rebel. We think if we get all our instructions directly from God we would obey because He would tell us the right thing to do all the time. Adam and Eve had only God to obey and that didn't work for them and neither will it work for us. We must obey sinners just like us. The question is, do we obey them if we are sure they are wrong? The problem is that we want our rights to the extent that we fight for them. If we are disobedient with anger our authority will overpower us. If our attitudes are right, we will have peace even if we have to suffer an unbiblical law.

This is why we must learn to love our enemies. With the right attitude we can love our persecutor. Grace only works when we have love. We are saved by grace because of Christ's love. Christ had the joy set before Him to endure the cross. In *Matthew 5:10-12* Jesus talks about the greatest joy a Christian can have. And that is being persecuted. It gives us a deeper reality of a better place to live.

There is no physical proof of God but He is as real as you want Him to be, depending on our faith. To try to convince someone that God exists doesn't bring proof. God leaves the proof to be Him coming inside our heart. That is why people think it is crazy to believe. They have no understanding in their minds. All they hear is religion not love, which is who God really is. This morning I prayed that God would give me a joy at the hospital. I had no idea what would happen until I met Gary. It was in a waiting room with about 10 other sad faces. Gary had it up to his neck with the organized church. I told him just because the church is not perfect doesn't mean you should blame the perfect God. That is not even logical. That was a good opener to get the others interested in what I had to say. I mention if we would acknowledge our sin the Scripture tells us we can become righteous. And when you become righteous, you will relate to a righteous God. Out of the whole bunch only Gary had a smile on his

73

face. God had us run into each other twice again before I left the hospital.

Our nation started with Christian principles. We are the only nation in the world that was started on Christian principles. That is why our nation prospered. At that time about 70 percent of our nation was spiritual and now about 85 percent of our country is not spiritual. All our laws were formed with Scriptural references.

Congress brought their Bibles to Congress and if a law was not backed up with a scriptural reference it was not voted into existence. Many today are ignorant of that fact.

The Jewish people are looking for a Messiah that would fight their battles for them. What Christ wants to do is to fight spiritual warfare; fighting off the spiritual darkness of this world. The fighting is inside of us and without God's help Satan will win. See *Ephesians 6:12*. God did fight the enemies for the Jewish people when they entered into the Promised Land but when the Israelites became disobedient their enemies conquered them.

The coming of Jesus brought us into the dispensation of Grace. Nobody can understand grace until it gives him or her Salvation but that is only the beginning. As we grow in Christ we can find out that we can love our enemies. God gave the Jews a command to kill their enemies. They were able to conquer one nation after another. As long as they obeyed the Lord there was victory.

We do not kill our enemies any longer but now we are told to love our enemies. Yet many Christians do not think that is possible, so they are still living by the law of the Old Testament.

Then the Jews started to lose their battles because of their disobedience. It started with the Babylonians, then the Romans, and in recent years continued with Hitler killing over 6 million Jews. The Jewish people lost their homeland twice and were slaughtered by their enemies. Many Jews came to the United States where many of them left their religion. They do not think God is on their side any longer. They do not see Jesus as their Messiah even though Jesus came as a Jew and only had his ministry among the Jews. The people love Jesus but the Jewish leaders were jealous so had Jesus crucified. Since Christ died they figured that He could not have been their Messiah. When Jesus resurrected He never appeared to non-believers. They thought it gave them the right not to believe. This has continued for more than 2,000 years.

That will soon change because of us Gentiles being disobedient the Lord will re-commission the Jewish people.

Many Christians are the same way, when something happens they will hold it against God. The Bible calls that tempting God. Some people even blame God for what He allows. "God why did you take my baby? And why did my wife get cancer?"

I witnessed to a Muslim at a train station. I asked a question: "Do you serve a righteous God?" He couldn't answer that question but after I explained what it meant he accepted Jesus. My explanation was to be righteous, one must love his enemies.

Disobedience starts by wanting things to satisfy ourselves. We become disobedient in three areas: immorality, riches, and the pride of life. This is the problem in raising children when they become disobedient, do parents express love to them? Even disciplining them must be in love or the wrong attitude will come out. But as far as a child is concerned, he or she has to learn love. Love is giving but a child wants. "When I was a child I spoke as a child, I thought as a child." A child is rich in faith but he must learn love from his parents, even when they are disciplining the child. But a child is rich in faith. "Except you have the faith of a child you shall in no way enter into the kingdom of heaven."

The Bible says to praise your children when they do well and discipline them in love when they do wrong. A child has not sinned until he can understand what is right and then rebels against what he knows is right. *James 4:17* If the parents practice love with each other and to their children, when the children grow up they will not depart from the Lord. The best reward God can give us is His presence within us. The Bible says prove me and see if I don't pour you out a blessing. It is the spirit of God in us that fills us with righteousness, which is to set the example for children.

Every time a child is right, praise him and give him a reward. When they are wrong parents must correct them in love. Correcting a child in anger only allows the child to accept anger and other wrong attitudes. The only way to get angry is to love the person and hate the sin. It is not human nature to separate sin from the person and that is why we get angry with the person. To us sin is the person. No! Sin is Satan. We resist Satan but love the sinner.

If you don't have the right attitude, do not punish your children until your attitude is right. But it is important to punish the child as soon as they are disobedient. Don't criticize when you see a child doing something wrong. It is easy to be frustrated. You need to tell them in love so they will become like you. A mother will have wisdom when she has love. A good way to correct a child is by asking a question—Do you think that was right?

Love brings wisdom and knowledge gives you facts. Knowledge will puff up a person and love edifies. We know that the commission of evangelism was handed over to the Gentiles because of the disobedience of the Jewish people. Their anger toward Jesus was expressed in wanting Him dead. It will not be long before the Gentiles lose the commission of evangelizing. At that time the commission will pass back to the Jewish nation. (*Revelation 7 and 14*)

When Jesus arose from the dead He never appeared to the ones who killed Him. That includes us until we are saved. We will never find Jesus in our sins. This is why we must continue to confess our sins. If we miss just one day in intimacy with Jesus we will think a daily relationship is not necessary and there will be unconfessed sin.

In the last days the commission will be handed back to the Jewish people because of the disobedience of the Gentile church. This will happen just before the total destruction of the earth. Many Christians think the rapture will come at any time. If it does, not many Church people will be caught up. The church is in apostasy and things are getting worse daily. The Christian thinks that our government is in sin. That is true but the church living in sin is the real problem.

According to many scholars the rapture will take place, but when? In the last fifty years there has been a constant falling away and today only a small percentage of people remain in the church and the church is far from being pure. Christians have many interpretations of the Book of Revelation. I believe many of the events are right but each interpretation has different timing for the events.

For example, everyone knows the prophecy that the Jewish people would return to their homeland but the time element was in diversity that is until the event happened. But when the Jews did return to their homeland the Scripture verified that was the time the Jews would return, but the timing went unnoticed until it happened.

I believe any interpretation of the Bible among Bible believing Christians differs because each interpretation is mostly an assumption in human intelligence. Yet most Christians have their doctrine as their main stress over the commands of Christ.

When I was the evangelical coordinator for the Billy Graham Crusade in West Africa the biggest problem was in doctrinal differences. Churches believed that their doctrine had superiority so they didn't endorse the crusade. Doctrine is important but if it hinders a Christian's fellowship how can it be justified? All wars have been justified but did war benefit society? If doctrine is from a cult we should have no fellowship with them, but is it right not to accept other fundamental denominations?

When I was saved in 1964 I saw doctrinal differences separating Christians. I had to shelf any attempt to do anything about it as a new Christian, but I knew it was destructive because it eliminated having love for one another. There is no sin that is not common to all mankind. I have confessed my sin. I believe the church has to examine itself and see how strong apostasy has entered into our country.

CHAPTER 90 WHY CHURCHES ARE HAVING SO MANY DIVISIONS

As already mentioned Satan tries to divide people by having them react badly to each other. This happens all the time. The big problem is when it happens in leadership.

God is above all but to obey God He has set up a chain of authority here on earth. In the armed forces we have the rank of authority such as the generals, the colonels, the captains, the lieutenants, the sergeants, corporals and the privates. In our civil government we have the president, vice-president, the speaker of the house etc. Then there is the State government starting with the governor and on down the line. In our educational system there is the principal, the teachers, right down to the students. In industry there is the president, the manager, supervisors, down to the workers. In the family God has the husband over the family, then the mother having authority over the children.

Every organization has ranks of authority. This authority is under God. The corruption comes when these authorities put themselves in the position of becoming like God. Of course they are tempted to do so by the god of this world. That is what Satan wanted for himself.

There are many places in the Bible that describe these chains of authority and we must obey them to be able to please God. The same way in the church. If we do not

obey our spiritual leaders we will be disobedient to God. Much of the time our authorities will be wrong according to our way of thinking. This is where God's love comes in. The common temptation of Satan is having us react badly to these authorities. This reaction will destroy our relationship to our leaders even more. This is where loving your enemy comes into focus.

If our leaders tell us to do something against the Bible, of course we should not obey. But again do we have a loving attitude? This is the example Jesus set for us. When the religious and the government leaders were wrong, Jesus took their wrong upon Himself. This includes all the people of the world. Whoever did wrong, Jesus took the wrong upon Himself. Jesus being the same yesterday, today, and forever, the time element didn't matter. Jesus died for people who came before Him and after Him, even to the end of the world.

Jesus proved his righteousness by being willing to suffer. We also need to have the right attitude in all things; we must be willing to suffer. *1 Peter 2:19-25.*

Nevertheless the main problem is not disobeying leaders but the leaders not being able to love the people under them. The main job of a church leader is to resolve problems in the church. All church divisions are caused by elders not being able to resolve problems. When a pastor cannot resolve problems of the people under him, he will justify himself that he is not the problem.

Pastors have a high rate of burnout today. Probably more than any other occupation. That is only for one reason. That is when the pastor tries to resolve sin and can't do it there is a reason for it. He can't love the person that is in rebellion. He will justify that the other party is in sin, and for this reason he can't see the sin in his own life. *Matthew 7:1-5*

The pastor's sin might seem to be smaller but is it really smaller? Jesus says differently. If the pastor can't cast the beam out of his own eye he will not see clearly to cast out the splinter from his brother's eye. The elders of a church cause all splits. If there is not a split it is because leadership knew how to rule.

When Jesus came as a Jew wanting to continue the Jewish people as the leaders of the new system under grace that system was to be under Jesus Himself. But the religious leaders killed Jesus because they thought He was starting His own ministry, which they believed because everyone was following Him. That was jealousy influencing them because that was not the intention of Jesus. After the Jews killed Jesus by the hands of the Romans they started to persecute the Christians.

The sad thing was that the new Christian leaders put themselves in the position equal with the civil law and they started to persecute Christians under them. Christianity broke up into two factions: the Catholics and the Orthodox. These leaders had fighting among themselves for years and many were killed.

Then came The Inquisition, when the leaders killed or imprisoned those who had beliefs not in complete unity with the church authorities.

Next the Reformation took place and fighting started many years of war. About 80 million Christians have been murdered at the hands of Christian leaders since the time of Christ.

When power is given to the organized church, religion becomes unrighteous. To become righteous one must confess his sins. In *First John 1:9* it says: "If we confess our sins God is faithful to forgive us of our sins and cleanse us from all unrighteousness." To be greatest of all we must become a servant of all. Church leadership is just the opposite of secular leadership. Education has taken preeminence where knowledge becomes more important than character quality.

Most all in Christianity today believe that we are living in the last church age of the Laodicean Church. This era of time ushers in the apostate church. This is the age of a great

falling away of the church and it will bring about persecution like the world has never seen before. And if it follows past traditions, the persecution will be from civil and religious leaders. Whenever man is put in charge, in politics or religion, he will use his authority to do what he thinks is right.

A dictator assumes the power to do what he wants, and in the past dictators have caused much corruption. A democratic government has some power to do what it thinks is right, but when the people do not agree they will vote someone else into office.

The church is divided into many different groups today mainly because they disagree with each other. But in most cases the government has restricted the power of religion controlling the government to the extent of denying Biblical principles.

But there are exceptions like the Islamic countries, but these countries are in disagreement with each other.

The question is how can God being righteous have His love abound, if it can't be by the civil government or organized religion? God still tells us to obey our leaders, yet man's leadership is not the answer.

I believe the answer is to have God come into our lives so God Himself will give us love, joy, and peace within ourselves. We do this not by fighting our government or our church but by letting these institutions see God in us.

Daniel was captured and was made a slave but he loved the people he served. In return God gave Daniel power to bring a wicked nation under the influence of a righteous God.

There is an old saying that things must get worse before they can get better. God lived up to that by allowing Himself to die in the hands of the wickedness of men in the world He created.

In remembering my life in Christ, I discovered after many years that I had something in my personality which was the same as I had in my life before I accepted Christ. That is disagreement with others when

I thought they were wrong. I didn't learn to be disagreeable as a Christian, but the habit was carried over from my old life. You can review my story again and you will see how I reacted in disagreement in many situations.

It is true that God forgives us of all our sins at the time we receive Christ. Why is it that we continue to commit the same sins? It is because we have formed bad habits as we grow up and they carried over into our Christian life. If habits were not carried over into our Christian life, and if we are not growing in Christ it would be easy to form other bad habits even as a Christian. Good and bad will follow us all through this life.

The challenge God gives us in the Christian life is for us to break these old habits. To stop drinking and smoking was easy for me because they were miracles. When God gives us a miracle we thank Him for that and try not to brag about it. Out of ten lepers who were healed only one thanked Jesus. The other nine went and bragged about what happened because after a miracle like that, nobody can keep silent.

There are, however, habits that tormented me for years. One of which is myself reacting badly to people I disagreed with.

If there is any one thing that destroys love, it is disagreement that gets out of hand. The destruction may not happen immediately, but over a period of time it will destroy friendships and marriages.

Most Christians believe that the church has entered into the period of apostasy. God loves everyone, but not everyone will go to heaven. Straight is the gate that leads to eternal life and few there be that find it. Below is a study on love:

There is no such thing as love at first sight, because beauty, riches, and popularity are attractions but not genuine love. There will be no marriages in heaven, as we know marriage in this present world.

Marriage in heaven is not restricted to couples. The bride is all of God's people. In heaven, romance is no longer an enjoyment; it will be replaced with God's love, a force not known to the natural man. It is pure love that unites and creates harmony in all of God's people.

Pseudo love can be part of a marriage. It is called love, but it is so easily connected with lust. Love is giving to others and lust is wanting for yourself. God so loved the world that He gave His Son to die. Lust is so strong that it can destroy. Lust is so close to love and yet they are opposites.

CHAPTER 91 TO COMMUNICATE WITH GOD

God created us in His image. A little child is still tender in that image and except we become as a little child, we will not enter into the Kingdom of God. It is interesting the word "Image," means likeness. The word "imagine" means to form a mental picture and the word "imagination" means to imagine something not seen. It is so easy to have a child believe in God. I believe it is because of their imagination. Their minds have not developed to understand things logically by their intellectual knowledge. For an adult, communication with God must be the same way, not by intellectualism but by us visualizing. To visualize means to form a mental image. So imagination and visualization are about the same thing. That is how we become as a little child, we humble ourselves and let the Holy Spirit be in control and not our intellect. God is a spirit and there is no knowledgeable proof of the spirit so God has us to visualize the things of God as a child would imagine things in their imaginary world. *John 4:24* "God *is* a Spirit: and they that worship him must worship *him* in spirit and in truth," *Matthew 18: 3-6 Mark 9:35-37*, and *Luke 18:19*. All these Scriptures say: if you do not come as a little child you shall not enter into the kingdom of God.

The spirit is the first part of us that receives salvation. The next part to reach is our mind and that is where the problem starts. God gives Satan our mind as his starting place for temptation so is it any wonder we all have a struggle in our thought life? When we fall into temptation, it seems like Satan is stronger than God. All sin is developed in the mind. The good thing is that God will not let us be subjected to any more than we can take. Come to think about it, we do not have to fall into temptation to be overcome in weakness and distress. Jesus had angels come and minister to Him when He was tempted in the wilderness.

As a person matures he becomes subject to the spirits of the world through knowledge which is part the tree of knowledge of good and evil. In the same way a Christian also needs to humble himself. *1 John 4:1* "Beloved, believe not every spirit, but try the spirits whether they are of God: because many false prophets are gone out into the world."

Religion has many different spirits today so we must cast out thoughts that are not of Christ. There are many false spirits in the world but only one righteous spirit. It is so easy for wrong spirits to enter into the mind and have them mix with the spirit of God when the information of what God gives us in our spirit is transferred to our mind. That is why the scripture says: "let this mind be in you which also is in Christ Jesus." The mind and the spirit of Christ are the same in oneness. Also the mind and the spirit of Christ can't sin. The spirit in us is without sin but the mind is subject to temptation and sin. Our thought life will betray us. The first thing I need to do is to love God with my spirit and then my mind.

Satan doesn't prevent us from having the truth but he tries to mix in little lies to distort the truth that the Holy Spirit gives us. It is the great scholars that have given us doctrines down through the years. The problem is when scholars have different interpretations. I ask myself, could this be of Satan's tree of knowledge. Maybe this is why Christians that seem to be less gifted are more necessary. See *First Corinthians 12:23*. "The less honorable bestow more abundant

honor." That means my mind must be free from conflict or I can have a nervous breakdown. Remember Jesus chose some uneducated men as disciples. Peter was one of them and he became a leader.

The word 'One' in the following scriptures means the same way for all. That all Christians would be of one spirit. *Ephesians 4:3-6* "Endeavouring to keep the unity of the Spirit in the bond of peace. [4] *There is* one body, and one Spirit, even as you are called in one hope of your calling; [5] One Lord, one faith, one baptism, [6]One God and Father of all, who *is* above all, and through all, and in you all."

The below Scriptures say we can be of the same spirit whether we are a Gentile or a Jew and no matter where we are geologically. *Ephesians 2:17- 18* "And came and preached peace to you which were afar off, and to them that were nigh. [18]For through Him we both have access by one Spirit unto the Father."

I believe in a cult or in other religions deception can get control of our spirit. See *John 17:23* we should be one with Jesus and with one another in the spirit. Being one with Christ means that God has control of our spirit, soul and body. This includes our will, hearts, minds, thoughts, strength and our emotions. The most important thing is getting daily instructions in righteousness for daily directions. *1 Thessalonians 5:23* "And the very God of peace sanctify you wholly and I pray God your whole spirit, soul and body be preserve blameless unto the coming of our Lord Jesus Christ. *Philippians 1:27* "Only let your conversation be as it becometh the gospel of Christ: that whether I come and see you, or else be absent, I may hear of your affairs, that you stand fast in one spirit, with one mind striving together for the faith of the gospel." Christians having the same spirit should have the same mind also, to come together in oneness.

There is only one truth. This means absolute truth. The same yesterday, today and forever. The very last verse of Phil. 2:16

says that we need to let the truth enter into our mind where Satan makes his entrance. He doesn't take the truth from us but he will mingle his lies with the truth to cause a variation that is not completely wrong but sufficient to cause others to react. We see this in our doctrinal positions. Satan knows Doctrine is an important issue. Doctrinal differences are a big cause of disobedience. Not so much that churches have different doctrine but that doctrine in many cases is not giving Christians the same compatibility. Jesus accused the spiritual leaders of being disobedient even though they were knowledgeable of the law. Jesus told the people to do what they say but not what they do. Good doctrine is not sufficient. Our good doctrine may be partially from Satan. I can't depend on my mind only or it will destroy my relationship with other Christians in my own church. It can also destroy a marriage. Because it was in the mind, Satan destroyed Adam's and Eve's relationship with the God that created them. This is explained in DENOMINATIONALISM below.

The following Scriptures tell us that it is the spirit of God that reveals the truth. Comparing ourselves with others is unwise but to compare our spirit with God's spirit is what we were designed to do. In verse 16, our mind becomes God's mind only after we have the spirit of God.

1 Corinthians 2:9-16
Verse 9 "But as it is written, Eye hath not seen, nor ear heard, neither have entered into the heart of man, the things which God hath prepared for them that love him."
Verse 10 "But God hath revealed *them* unto us by his Spirit: for the Spirit searcheth all things, yea, the deep things of God."
Verse 11 "For what man knoweth the things of a man, save the spirit of man which is in him? Even so the things of God knoweth no man, but the Spirit of God."
Verse 12 "How we have received, not the spirit of the world, but the spirit which is of God; that we might know the things that are freely given to us of God."

Verse 13 "Which things also we speak, not in the words which man's wisdom teacheth, but which the Holy Ghost teacheth; comparing spiritual things with spiritual."
Verse 14 "But the natural man receiveth not the things of the Spirit of God: for they are foolishness unto him: neither can he know *them*, because they are spiritually discerned."
Verse 15 "But he that is spiritual judgeth all things, yet he himself is judged of no man."
Verse 16 "For who hath known the mind of the Lord, that he may instruct him? But we have the mind of Christ."

ONENESS IN CHRIST AMONG CHRISTIANS

Every Christian should think and live the same way. Jesus said that He was the way, the truth and the life and we should have the Gospel as our guidance. We should examine and meditate on everything Jesus did and said. All Scripture is inspired but not all Scripture is for doctrine. All major doctrines must be backed up with what Jesus backed up with His Life or Words. For example the deity of Christ was backed up by what Jesus did more than what He said. We as adults need to humble ourselves as a little child not only for salvation but also every time we get into conflict. A mother in Wichita, Kansas, told me that her son came home one night after a fight with his best friend. She told me she tried to comfort her son but it was to no avail. The next morning after breakfast her son said, "I'm going to see Tommy." The mother said, "Isn't that the one you had a fight with last night and you came home angry?" The son said, "No, Tommy is my best friend."

DENOMINATIONALISM

Denominationalism came from very intelligent people down through history. John Calvin and John Wesley lived in overlapping time spans but never met each other until one day Calvin was in the area where Wesley lived so he stopped in to see him. They had a warm greeting but it didn't last long. They spent all day discussing doctrine and they couldn't agree with each other. The love they had when they met wasn't there when they departed.

For the first 300 years after the ascension there was persecution, so Christians met in small groups. As evangelists traveled from group to group they were amazed at the extreme doctrinal differences and they wanted the Christians to be united together with the same doctrine.

Nevertheless, during those 300 years the Christians evangelized most of the Roman Empire. About 7 percent of the empire were converted. This was real Christianity. They were willing to die as a mother is willing to die for her child. They didn't have different doctrine because of disagreement of others, but within themselves they were in full agreement. I believe God allows different doctrines in the autonomous church. That means each group of believers should search the Scriptures for their own doctrine. When I was in Africa there were people in the fellowship that had several wives before coming into salvation. This problem should be resolved by the church coming together in prayer and fasting. A Church that doesn't have that problem has no need for a doctrine on this issue. In America we have what is called the statements of faith. This is general doctrines that all Christian churches should have. To have one general church that controls Christianity around the world will never work. History has proven this. In 70 AD when Jerusalem was destroyed the Jerusalem counsel did not have control over all Christianity any longer. The apostles were scattered and had individual groups independent from each other and no more one central church until the Roman Empire made it that way again, which has continued to this day. This has caused denominationalism, which has separated Christianity into factions.

CHRISTIANITY CONTROLLED BY THE ROMAN EMPIRE

When Constantine made Christianity an official religion of the Roman Empire, it became a State religion which had the power to kill others that believed differently.

By the Roman Empire the New Testament was canonized. Two of the strongest criteria's were: choosing godly men and second, their writings had to be in agreement with each other, so doctrine would be unified. This has given to us in the center reference Bible that states all the common Spiritual references throughout the New and the Old Testament. This didn't work because educated scholars had different interpretations of the Bible. Within recent years these center references have been discarded and educated men were chosen to be pastors. The Bible teaches that a pastor has many qualifications and the most important ones were to practice discipleship and to keep unity in the church by guarding the flock against evil men especially from inside the church. See Titus 1:6-16. These qualifications have been discarded today.

The result was that Christianity was built on intellectualism rather than on discipleship. Since that time, Christianity had made their efforts to continue training Christian leaders with education but without discipleship as Jesus did.

SATAN IS IN CONTROL OF THE TREE OF KNOWLEDGE OF GOOD AND EVIL

God gave Satan his power in the tree of the knowledge of good and evil. This tree was off-limits to Adam and Eve. Satan tries to give temptation in having us believe we can be like God by knowing what is right and wrong. Adam and Eve were deceived by Satan in disobedience to God. The first deception was they didn't need God if they knew what was right and wrong in every situation and second, Satan doesn't give everyone the same information of what is right and wrong, which causes conflicts in every area of life in the world. Conflicts in what is right and wrong are the root of all wars, and they say all wars are centered on religion.

Satan has us justify our thoughts on what we think is right. Every battle on the face of this earth has been justified by both sides but in different ways. Since the beginning of keeping records there have been over 20,000 battles. In the Second World War, there were several hundred battles before the war was won. How many battles take place in marriages before the war is over. And when it is over, which side has won?

CHRIST IS THE MEDIATOR OF THE TRUE CHURCH

Every religion on this earth, including Christianity, has had unrighteous acts. And in organized religion we find unrighteous men. The church leaders are not our mediators but it is Jesus who is the same mediator for us all to bring the church in His control with Love and power to draw all men and women to Christ. Our biggest problem is drawing others to Christ in our own church. The true church started with Jesus who taught by discipleship perfect love. When God's love is rejected we will be like Judas. Remember, to love God and to love one another is part of the same commandment. *Matthew 22:37-40*

When the discipleship training was terminated the disciples became apostles so they could start the process all over again. We will be bystanders, followers or disciples. The bystanders are the world. The followers are ones that want to hear the Gospel and be followers but the disciples were obedient to Christ and did what they were taught for three years. "Many are called but few are chosen." *Matthew 20:16.* The only chosen ones were the disciples.

The intellectual leaders were the ones who put Jesus to death. The more power the church has, the more it will justify itself in forcing discipline on others. Doctrine differences caused many killings since the first coming of Christ. Over 70 million Christians were killed by other Christians that had the power of the government.

State religion started in the third century and continued until the United Sates was formed without religion controlling the government, but Christians in the government controlling the laws of the land. Sad to say that hasn't continued to happen. The tragedy started in 1957 when more people percentage-wise went to church since the beginning of our nation. Since 1957 there has been a slow decrease until the present time. Now more people are not going to church since our nation was formed. Tell me, is it the government's fault or the fault of Christians? In my travels, each church does not think it is their fault but they know that the problem exists.

Our country was formed by Christians in England and Europe who wanted religious freedom. There were about 10 different religious groups that settled in the New World but each of them had doctrinal differences and each thought they were right and each one of them wanted preeminence in setting up our new government. This brought the country to a standstill for a while. Roger Williams had the solution and was going to be deported but he escaped and lived with the native Indians for a while. Roger Williams made himself known again when the real struggle began. It was his advice that brought the government and the church to an agreement to prohibit any one church from having preeminence in the government.

Separation from Church and State is that no one church would control the government but Christians would be in the government to make Christian laws. The church will never have the perfect doctrine but the church can have perfect love, which is to love others who disagree with you in doctrine. This is the basis of the righteousness of Jesus. He loved everyone so much that he died for being right. Jesus did not react or complain on the cross. Christianity is not being righteous by having right doctrine. I believe God made the Scriptures ambiguous to expose the nature of man. The Scripture is the Word of God and only those who want God could understand. To others the Bible is a book of contradictions or just a history book.

The USA was the only world power to start a government on Christian principles. We never changed our form of government but now education is in control and not Christianity. In fact our government has taken control of Christianity. Christianity started education with teaching God-given principles. Now education is nothing more than Satan having his power in the tree of knowledge of good and evil, that God put off-limits to Adam and Eve. As Adam and Eve were deceived so is the church today. It was the different doctrines that had Christians opposing each other. Today Christianity is at its lowest point of influence for two reasons: first, we are not loving people who come against us, and second, we have the lowest percentage rating of people attending church than ever before, since the beginning of our country. The sad thing is that the church has lost its influence in our own country. We need to return to how Jesus started training disciples. It was hard work being out in public daily as Jesus did and taught His disciples. Maybe because of the hard work, leaders found it easy to have the public come to them, but it doesn't work that way.

THE BIBLE IS DIFFICULT TO UNDERSTAND

For centuries the church refused to put the Bible in the hands of the people because it is hard to understand. It was the clergy who had the ability to interpret the Scriptures. This put a separation between clergy and laity. Finally it was concluded that the Bible was for all of God's people. With the Holy Spirit giving direction from within a person, all mankind would be able to understand. There are two aspects for understanding. One is for doctrine and the other is for guidance for the struggles in everyday life. This is time-consuming but God promised to give us a joy in His presence. A fellow in love enjoys spending time with his would-be bride. Jesus is our bridegroom and we are told to pray or talk to Him without ceasing. Also in everything we do we should do all the glory of God. The only difference between clergy and laity is the clergy would be the pastor to shepherd the sheep, which is the laity. This is called discipleship. After the training the person who was the disciple will now be the pastor, able to disciple another person. I do not see this in the church today.

MAN DIDN'T CONTINUE WHAT JESUS STARTED

After Christ ascended into heaven, famous scholars have studied the Bible to find the perfect interpretation. But all those scholars did more to divide the church than to unify the church. The church still uses educated men for doctrine but also for church leadership. I have talked to educated Christians. They were so happy to graduate to get into the actual experience. Then they found out that starting a church was more of a struggle than getting the education.

Today everything is of man's knowledge, which has prevented the church from reproducing itself. Spiritual knowledge is not much better if we do not obey God's Word. Jesus calls them hypocrites. What was the educational level of the 12 disciples? Some of them could not read and write and yet with some hard training they were able to continue Christianity and spread it to become the largest religion of the world. Today many Christian leaders are hindering Christianity from spreading because their position is one of leadership and not servant-hood. "If any want to be greatest let him be servant of all." *See Mark 9:34-35.*

BACK TO THE FOUNDATIONS

When things are not working we should go back to the foundation to see how Jesus started Christianity. The Bible gives us four Gospels, yet the church prefers tradition over the way Jesus started the church. Every time Jesus used the word "church," what did He mean? Jesus use the word "church" only two times.

- *Matt 16:18* Jesus said: "My Church"
- *Matt 18:17* Jesus said: "Tell it to the church"

In both cases He meant, people. Jesus was talking to people, not a building.

In every place the Bible uses the word "preaching" it refers to speaking to the public while training His disciples. When the word "teaching" is used it refers to speaking to His disciples.

TRAINING OTHERS IN DISCIPLESHIP

Ephesians chapter 4 says we should endeavor to express love to keep unity, and be training apostles, prophets, evangelist and pastor and teachers. Today, the best the church knows is to send believers to Bible colleges or seminaries to receive spiritual knowledge. In many cases this hinders Christian maturity because the individual is so busy in his studies that he doesn't have time for his personal devotions to the Lord. Whether it is secular or spiritual knowledge the Bible says that knowledge will make man proud but love will edify each other. *See 1 Corinthians 8:1.*

WHY DO CHRISTIANS STRESS DOCTRINE?

Doctrine doesn't change a person to make them obedient. If anything it seems that doctrine builds fences. At the VA hospital I met a lady who was so unhappy. I said, "Cheer up, God loves you." That statement opened her up to share her life of 40 years of marriage. She said that she was a Protestant and her husband was a Catholic. She never wanted to go to his church and he didn't want to go to her church. I told her that I knew how strong tradition was, but asked her, "Couldn't you pray and read the Bible together in your house and start a new tradition?"

If the Bible was only for doctrine why is it that the wisdom of man is always coming up with new doctrines? And why are the doctrines of fundamental churches coming up with different interpretations of what the Bible says. And a number of these interpretations have opposite meanings. Justified beliefs can limit one's ability to understand spiritual principles of how great God's love is.

I questioned why there are so many different doctrines immediately after I found salvation. As I matured in the faith I started to hang out with people of different doctrines. I have tried the Holiness, the Calvinistic and the Pentecostal persuasions. They all seemed to be nice people, that is, until they talked against the doctrines of others. Nevertheless I was able to work with them all. That is, after I got over my denominational prejudices. God showed me that righteous people will go to heaven, not people with righteous doctrine. Doctrine and obedience are two different aspects. The Jewish people had right doctrine and God said they were disobedient. Jesus said in Matthew 5 that unless our righteous exceed the righteous of the Scribes and the Pharisees we will not enter the kingdom of God.

THE CHURCH HAS A BIGGER PROBLEM

The church should be teaching obedience. Obedience is the application of God's Word. In *2 Timothy 3:16* the Bible says doctrine is only one part of what the Bible is profitable for. This verse mentions three areas of application which every person is aware of because God allows problems in our everyday activities so we will go to Bible for help. The Scriptures will show us where we are wrong, how to correct those wrongs, and receive daily instructions in righteousness so we will do the right things when planning our day and every day.

When God's spirit is uniting with our spirit, God's Word becomes an instruction book. We can understand what God's spirit is telling us concerning the situation we are in, then God's word becomes alive. The definition of the Word of God has two meanings. One is Logos and the other is

Rhema. Logos is what the Word means literally, which has one meaning which is for doctrine. Rhema means utterance or listening to what God tells us, so we can obey Him. This can be different for each person because we must visualize God directing from inside our spirit. This is how God gives instructions and his instruction is called the Word of God. This method is used for personal devotions, family devotions or any group wanting God's help by searching the Scriptures together for any problem. Most Christians must get into problems over their heads before they ever search the Bible for directions. But if this is done every day we have practice in hearing God's voice: *John 10:27* "My sheep hear my voice and I know them and they follow me." It should be done daily to practice discernment.

JESUS TRAINED HIS DISCIPLES TO MIMIC HIM

We think we must use forced discipline on people so they will obey us. The government and our armed forces use discipline because they do not know any other way. The reason Jesus spent so much time daily with His disciples was to love them and because He wanted them to mimic Him. Love is contagious.

The government and our armed forces use forced discipline because they can't make it a law to love one another. Only God knows the heart. He first loved us by being willing to suffer. We return His love by hearing His voice in obedience. This is why God is love and stresses love as the solution of all our problems. All the law and the prophets hinges on love. If you love your brother there is no reason for falling from grace. There is no fear in love. *2 Timothy 1:7* "for God has not given us the spirit of fear, but of power, and of love, and of a sound mind."

THE IMPORTANCE OF DISCIPLESHIP AND DISCIPLINE

Jesus made no attempt to set rules for discipleship or to force discipline on His disciples. This may sound strange but first, the word "disciple" is not a verb but a noun and every time it is used in the Gospels it is a noun. That means Jesus didn't teach discipleship but He showed it to them by being with them every day for 3 years.

The word discipline is not found once in the New Testament. Jesus never disciplined Judas even though Judas was a thief and a would-be murderer. Instead Jesus allowed Judas to continue being a disciple and the treasurer but the Lord still loved Judas as He did the other disciples. What happens when one lies to the Holy Spirit? Ananias and Sapphira found this out but didn't live to tell about it. They were involved in secret sin which is a common thing these days in the church. When the church was pure the Lord didn't allow sin to happen. We now see secret sin being so common that you can get away with it but sin will find you out. The grace of God allows us to live in sin but at the same time God's love wants us to discipline ourselves. When someone loves a child, the child wants to mimic you. The sad thing is that they will also mimic you when you are angry and practice sin.

Jesus chose to show discipleship by His example and He chose to have discipline by temperance. The dictionary definition of temperance is: To control oneself in over-indulgence of any kind. It's called self-discipline. Jesus was wanting Judas to discipline himself. When Judas's sin found him out, it was too late.

Jesus had the fruit of the Spirit in His own life and showed His disciples that the fruit of the spirit can replace the manifestations of the flesh. The acts of the flesh are under three areas: immorality, materialism and pride. They should be replaced by the fruit of the spirit. They are: love, joy, peace, patience, gentleness, goodness, faith, meekness and temperance or self-control.

The fruits of the spirit were designed so that you can't have one without the others. For example: you can't have love without self-control. This is why Christianity is based on love. If you have love, you have everything needed for the Christian life and remember that includes self-control. But if you can't love your enemy, you can't begin to understand God's love. God's righteousness was accomplished by dying. We can only love our enemy by dying to the old nature. This takes suffering, which is related to Christ's death. *1 Timothy 1:11-12* "If we are dead with Him we will also live with Him. If we suffer, we shall also reign with Him."

JESUS LIVED HIS LIFE TO TEACH OTHERS PERSONALLY

Jesus had to spend much of His time with His disciples so that they would mimic Him. This is why parents must spend much of their time with their children. Their qualification in doing this is to live a Christ-like life themselves. Of course parents are not perfect, but God has a way to cover the imperfections and they become righteous again: *1 John 1:9* "If we confess our sins, He is faithful and just to forgive us our sins, and to cleanse us from all unrighteousness."

Jesus didn't preach to His disciples but He preached to the multitudes while His disciples listened. A pastor preaching to his congregation doesn't do very much good. The information goes in one ear and out the other. Most people can't discipline themselves to see how the message applies to themselves. Living righteously takes away the joy that the flesh offers. Self-discipline lets us see the joy we can have in the spirit. It takes an example to show others Discipline. When Jesus preached to others the disciples saw the power in love which will heal physically and spiritually. This was what drew the disciples to Jesus. His suffering did it. "If I be lifted up I will draw all Men unto me." *John 12:32* "And if I be lifted up from the earth, I will draw all men unto me."

CHURCH IS THE PEOPLE NOT A BUILDING

If you took away four walls of the church we would be in public. But for some reason most of the Gospel in kept within the four walls. In fact even when the people leave, the Gospel is still within the four walls because the people have not been trained to share the love of Christ with others.

SWEAR NOT AT ALL

This commandment "Swear not at all" is in *Matthew 5:34.* Jesus gave us the Sermon on the Mount to show us that a commitment to be faithful to God and others is a very important doctrine. One can't be faithful without total commitment. A commitment to Jesus can seem like bondage at first but the joy of always being with Jesus has no comparison with what the world has to offer. The commitment of being married takes much more discipline than the single person. Commitment to Jesus is as a marriage and it will take much discipline. Discipline is part of the fruit of the spirit and we should practice the fruit on a daily basis.

Matthew 5:36 "Neither shalt thou swear by thy head, because thou canst not make one hair white or black. [37] But let your communication be, Yea, yea; Nay, nay: for whatsoever is more than these cometh of evil."

Swearing is telling people that you tell the truth. Jesus tells us to show others by our faithfulness in keeping our word. Jesus made an emphasis not to swear in any way. People swear only to try to convince others that they are telling the truth and most of the time that means little. But what Jesus says is to be faithful in what you tell people you will do or not do. God tells us that He is faithful in the Scriptures three times for each time He tells us to be faithful once in the Scriptures. It is God's way of showing us how important faithfulness is. Jesus was faithful to His disciples much more than He expected them to be faithful. *2 Tim 2:2.* When people make promises to me but do not fulfill their promises I see that I can't trust them in the future. That used to discourage me but now I see how Jesus loved me when I was unfaithful. I can't count the times people tell me that they will meet me in church but never show up. Jesus wants us as disciples to return as a little child so we would have others see Jesus in us and want to be faithful.

Matthew 18:3-6 "And said, Verily I say unto you, except you be converted, and become as little children, you shall not enter into the kingdom of heaven. ⁴ Whosoever therefore shall humble himself as this little child, the same is greatest in the kingdom of heaven. ⁵ And whoso shall receive one such little child in my name receiveth me. ⁶ But whoso shall offend one of these little ones which believe in me, it were better for him that a millstone were hanged about his neck, and that he were drowned in the depth of the sea."

WHAT IS JUDGING?

Judging is telling someone they are wrong, but then they react to you. It is our reaction back to them that shows we are judging. Our reaction destroys our love for our enemies. We must judge others to eliminate sin but we need spiritual maturity in love to do so. *1 Corinthians 2:15:* "But he that is spiritual judgeth all things, yet he himself is judged of no man." With God's love the rebuked person will not react to us. It is the immaturity that causes all the church division these days and just about every church has divisions, and it is because of a lack of love for the sinner. Jesus loves the sinner and hates his sin. Jesus loves everyone. That means if we can't love the sinner, then we will not be able to love people in the church either. Jesus loves me when I still have sinned. If I remind myself of this, I will think of others differently.

Jesus rebuked Peter to his face but Peter didn't react back. Jesus loved Peter, that is why Peter didn't react back. But nevertheless Jesus did not make it a habit to rebuke His disciples because He wanted them to learn self-control. The number of

times you must show love in order to rebuke is without number. This is why Jesus says to forgive 70 times 7. *Mattthew 18:22*

Jesus did judge the religious leaders at that time and they reacted back. In fact they reacted so much that they used their power to have Jesus crucified. But the reaction was necessary to show the sin of the spiritual leaders and to die for their sin as well as for our sins to prove Jesus loves us all. When leaders commit sin they must be rebuked because the church will be no better than the leaders, but to rebuke publicly it must be by at least two or three others in the church. *See 1 Timothy 5:18.* That is only when you rebuke an elder before the church. The pastor is human just like you and me and there is nothing wrong going to him personally and telling him in love where he did wrong. This is usually when the sparks fly. We must build ourselves up in our most holy faith, praying in the Holy Ghost. *Jude 20.* You will know when you are praying in the Holy Ghost. Don't jump the gun, as our human nature does.

When we learn from the Master, which is Christ or living Christ-like, we are to start our own work and separate from our teacher physically so we can be a master to others. You become a master after your discipleship training, but that gives you the ability to be a servant of all. When one becomes the head of hundreds of churches around the world he can become a dictator so easily. And everyone that does this sets up rules for everyone to obey. Jesus left His disciples so they could learn leadership on their own. If they didn't learn self-discipline when the Lord was with them it becomes harder as a leader.

Constantine started a general headquarters when he made Christianity legal in the Roman Empire. It was Constantine who made the decision to have a national conference and had all the Bishops attend at the government's expense.

Constantine killed his own brother and his wife because they disagreed with him. But by being the greatest in the Roman Empire it was legal for him. His mother told Constantine in order to repent he should build churches all over the Roman Empire. He did and he put in educated men to be pastors. The church became so corrupted that many left the Roman Empire to start monasteries all over Northern Africa, outside the Roman boundaries. Today they are finding monasteries by the thousands. I believe that was what gave Christianity respect. Even the Pope respected the monks for all their prayers and fasting. But the monks restricted priests from joining the monasteries because the Roman Empire had control over them. The reason why the ministry of monks didn't continue in the New World is because the word "Monk" means single ones, and the Christians believe it is the family that makes up the church.

At the time Christian men couldn't ask their families to start a pure church in the African desert, with temperatures of over 110 degrees in the middle of a desert. Jesus, not being married, did spend the first 40 days in the wilderness to fast and pray so there was good meaning behind what the monks did and it served a purpose at that time. I believe even married men should live at times like they have no wife and go into the desert and pray. *See 1 Corinthians 7:29.* It has been reported that some of these monks were the godliest people that lived because of their dedication to prayer and fasting.

CHAPTER 92 LOVE PROMOTES MAKING CHRIST KNOWN PUBLICLY

I did learn to be a witness for Christ but not in a life of complete victory. It was because of a bad habit that I never conquered. Others saw the problem but I was not able to accept it. It was my own rebellion. I either was excusing or accusing others of their sins. *Romans 2:15* "Which show the work of the law written in their hearts, their conscience also bearing witness, and their thoughts the mean while accusing or else excusing one another." Without love we will excuse others and let them continue to sin. If we accuse others, we

will tell others they are wrong. Without love there is no right way to deal with sin.

The problem is that there is no way to continue doing something where there is no joy. Everything that Jesus did we can do also. Our love for Jesus must be in everything we do. The secret is doing it with joy so we will want to continue doing it.

Colossians 3:17 "My brethren, count it all joy when you fall into divers temptations..." We are to resist Satan but not evil people. *Matthew 5:39* "But I say unto you do not resist them that are evil" *James 1:2 5* If Jesus is in us, just the thought of that should be joy. It is God living inside us as the hope of glory. Love, joy and peace are the first three parts of the fruit of the spirit, not lust, pleasure, and to conquer.

When I first started witnessing, I did it because I was commanded to do so. When we are in love with Jesus, we can do it because we want to do it. The Holy Spirit works inside of us and gives us His fruit. The fruit of the Spirit is: Love, joy, peace, patience, goodness, gentleness, faith, meekness and temperance. The love, joy, and peace give us purpose to live. The patience, goodness and gentleness are to show others that our love, joy, and peace are God given. The faith, meekness, and temperance are to bring our self into God's control. It took me a long time to become obedient to what would change me so I would draw people to God's love. Jesus had to suffer to draw people to Him. When I was willing to suffer for doing what was right, I started to have the joy that Jesus had. Jesus says if any two will agree on any one thing, it will be done for them. When there is no agreement the Holy Spirit is grieved and we will feel the same way.

While couples are dating the romance is so heavy there is little desire for the spiritual and if the spiritual is not there before marriage it will have its struggles after marriage. Because of our feelings, it is so easy to think that the love between man and woman is greater than God's love that

created marriage. It has to be deception to make anyone think that way. It seems in the following passages, you have to separate yourself from your compassion for each other to be serious about spiritual matters. But of course this has to be done in agreement.
1 Corinthians. 7:34 "There is a difference also between a wife and a virgin. The unmarried woman cares for the things of the Lord, that she may be holy both in body and in spirit: but she that is married cares for the things of the world, how she may please her husband..."
1 Corinthians 7:5 "Defraud not one the other, except it be with consent for a time, that you may give yourselves to fasting and prayer; and
come together again, that Satan tempt you not for your incontinence."

Lust is wanting something for yourself and this can be a problem in marriage when the spouse is not in the mood for sex. It takes more discipline to be married than being single. The Bible says that our body is not our own when married. This means that a husband has rights, but you can't fight for your rights. Jesus had no rights. See *Philippians 2.*

One time I met a married couple that was very active in ministry. I asked them how much did they pray for each other. To my surprise they both never even thought about praying for each other. Both husbands and wives need their own personal time with the Lord to make sure that their marriage needs the Lord to guard intimacy with each other. The husband's responsibility is to be the spiritual leader of the family.

Men and woman do not think alike. Men are not interested in knitting and women do not like to tinker in the garage. So each will do their "own thing" and there is no problem with that. Both are doing things that are necessary in organizing the household and both should praise each other for doing their part. Praises win each other's confidence when you are involved in different projects. As much as your children rebel,

parents need to look for times to praise them on a regular basis. If parents don't praise their children, their boyfriends or girlfriends will. Usually that is what starts tension in the family when the children become teenagers.

Luke 15:15-20 And He said unto them, go into all the world, and preach the gospel to every creature, [16] He that believeth and is baptized shall be save; but he that believeth not shall be dammed. [17] And these signs shall follow them that believe in my name shall they cast out devils, they shall speak with new tongues, [18] They shall take up serpents and if they drink any deadly thing, it shall not hurt them, they shall lay hands on the sick and they shall recover. [19] So then after the Lord had spoken unto them, He was received up into heaven, and sat on the right hand of God. [20] And they went forth, and preached everywhere, the Lord working with them and confirming the word with signs following. Amen.

Luke 18:15-17 And they brought unto him also infants, that He would touch them, but when his disciples saw it, they rebuked them. [16] But Jesus called him unto him, and said, suffer little children to come unto Me, and forbid them not, for of such is the kingdom of God. [17] Verily I say unto you, whosoever shall not receive the kingdom of God as a little child shall in no wise enter therein.
1 John 3:24 And he that keepeth his commandments dwelleth in him, and he in him. And hereby we know that he abideth in us, by the Spirit which he hath given us.

CHAPTER 93 FRUIT OF THE SPIRIT

Discipline is an important factor in the church, yet the word discipline is not mentioned once in the New Testament. Jesus did rebuke his disciples a few times but the word "disciple" is always used in the Gospels as a noun and the dictionary also classifies the word "disciple" only as a noun. That means Jesus didn't tell them what to do nor did He force discipline on them. The exceptions were onetime events. In everyday training Jesus showed discipleship and discipline to His disciples by the example of His own life. Jesus did it in love so His disciples would mimic Him. This is why Jesus spent most of His time with His disciples. We humans can't understand love because having the love of this world is not the love of God. Your love is where you spend most of your time. Here are some Scriptural facts about God's love.

First: To know God's love we must obey Him. *John 14:23* "Jesus answered and said unto him, if a man love me, he will keep my words, and the Father will love him, and make our abode with Him."

Second: To obey Jesus we must love one another. *John 15:7* "These things I command you that you love one another."

Third: Hate is the opposite of love and so having God's love the world will hate us. *John 15:18* "If the world hate you, you know that it hated Me before it hated you." The Pharisees hated Jesus because Christ's love had everyone following Him. Cain hated Abel because Abel's sacrifice was better. Jealousy produces hate.

Fourth: Human nature only knows the love that is in the world. One cannot have the love of the world at the same time as he has the love of God. *1 John 2:15* "love not the world neither the things that are in the world, if any man love the world, the love of the Father is not in him.

Fifth: The love of the world is considered as nothing but lust of the flesh and the eyes. *1 John 2:15-16* "Love not the world, neither the things that are in the world. If any man love the world, the love of the Father is not in him. For all that is in the world, the lust of the flesh and the lust of the eyes, and the pride of life."

The four Gospels are the starting place for Church discipline. Jesus trained his disciples to be like Himself. The 12 disciples had Jesus with them all day to show them the way. The only difference today is the Holy Spirit is living in us, to have us be like Jesus, which is far better but only with temperance.

Temperance is self-discipline and it is only effective in changing ourselves. Trying to change others is the world's way of forcing people to be righteous. Righteousness comes only by way of Jesus Christ and Jesus in us has to be in control by our Temperance. Mankind knows well the flaws in human nature and man's ways to deal with these are to bring others into obedience by force. The government enforces the law by incarceration. The armed forces use strict discipline and force. Employers control the employee from the time he punches in until he punches out. When angry, parents force discipline on their children. Church discipline without love has caused much bitterness in almost every church in the country. Much of the time church leadership is based on Biblical knowledge before virtue. *Second Peter 1: 5* says virtue comes before knowledge. Knowledge will make a person proud but love will edify.

1 Corinthians 8:1 "Knowledge puffed but love edifieth." Forced discipline doesn't work any better in the church than in any secular organization. Church divisions are the major reasons for people leaving the church. Every year since 1957, attendance has dropped from 65 percent of America attending church, to now only 14.5 percent and it is continuing to decrease. Disciplining Christians living in sin is mostly an act of accusing or excusing sin. *Romans 2:15* "which show the work of law written in their hearts, their conscience also bearing witness, and their thoughts, the mean while accusing or else excusing one another."

The answer to all these problems are found in the Gospels, not in the epistles. Jesus dealt with Judas in a very special way, which was without an argument but not without suffering. Jesus disciplined Judas in love but Judas failed to respond. We also can love our enemy. See chapters 88-93.

Christ wants obedience in His children. He compares marriage to Himself and His bride, the church. If we are obedient to Christ then our children will be obedient to us. See

Matthew 8:10. If a man obeys authority over him, then people under him will obey him. Also in *1 Corinthians 15*. The disobedience of the first Adam hands down sin but the righteousness of the second Adam, who is Jesus, hands down righteousness.

As the husband is the head of the wife in the same way Christ is the head of the church which is His disciples. *Ephesians 5:23* "For the husband is the head of the wife, even as Christ is the head of the church: and he is the savior of the body."

Christ didn't force obedience on His disciples. In the same way a husband should not force anything on his wife. He should love her and be an example for the whole family. *Ephesians. 5:28-29* "So ought men to love their wives as their own bodies, he that loves his wife, loves himself. For no man ever yet hates his own flesh, but nourishes and cherishes it, even as the Lord the church." The husband's duty is to love his wife as Jesus loved the church. This is a spiritual love that goes beyond the love of this world. See *Ephesians 3:19.*

Below are some spiritual areas that a husband should include, but the husband must first apply these disciplines in his own life in obedience to God's Word. If the husband does not have the fruit of the spirit, neither will he be an example for his family. The fruit of the spirit starts with love and ends with self-control. You can't have one fruit without the others. See *Galatians 5:22-23*. The noun "fruit" and the verb "is" are both singular. The fruit of the Spirit is nine things. That means they are all part of the same package.

Below are some ways a husband should spiritually be the head of his family as Jesus was the head of His disciples. Father and mother both should have discipleship with their children.

1. Daily time with his family in the Word and prayer.
2. Applying the Word to daily events with the family participating.
3. Memorizing a verse together weekly and quoting that verse every day that week at the start of daily devotions.
4. Meditate on Scripture to have the Holy Spirit in control.
5. Accountability in everyone's thought life. The family must be transparent.
6. Praying for the activities for each family member.
7. Witnessing as a family in public and inviting friends over for a meal.
8. Practice confessing sins during family devotions. Starting with the father setting the example.

If any man wants to preform discipleship on anyone he must have discipleship in his own family. Not having members of his own family in submission will disqualify a man from being an elder in the church. *1 Timothy 3:4* "One that rules well his own house, having his children in subjection with all gravity."

In a prior chapter I wrote about this following conversation I had while witnessing to a man:

The other day I was talking to a gentleman and he said that we need to know the truth. I asked him, what is the truth? He said that it depended on the situation. I told him the truth must be the same yesterday, today and forever. Without absolute truth there will be only arguments.

As I was having my morning devotions today I started thinking about how one resolves problems. The above man that I had the conversation with said that with the truth we would be able to resolve problems. That hit me strongly because that is exactly what I have been doing with others. Daily I have been getting others engaged in going over a verse a day to see what God was saying to us concerning problems that we wanted solutions for. If we believe that the Bible is absolute truth then by mediating on the Word daily we could have a solution to our problems by God Himself.

CHAPTER 94 APOSTASY IN THE BIBLE

From the book of Revelation we understand that we are living in the last church age which is known as the apostate age. Apostate or apostasy means a falling away from the church or not being loyal to God. This means complacency and disobedience. Complacency is self-satisfaction to worldly pleasures and disobedience is not following Christ's commands. These two things are related because one will be conformed to this world when disobedient to God.

How Jesus disciplined His disciples probably has never been a main function in the church. The word disciple is a noun and each time it is used in the New Testament it is used as a noun. This means that Jesus did not disciple his disciples or it would be changing the noun into a verb. Instead of forcing discipline on His disciples, Jesus showed his disciples. All they had to do was to watch and listen. The word discipline is closely related to disciple but it is not found once in the King James Bible. We do find the use of discipline in the world. Much of society has an understanding that human nature is corrupt so discipline is used to help resolved the problem.

For example: the government has laws and forces the law by discipline. The armed forces have even stronger discipline. I never saw a sergeant with motherly love. Our educational system has rules and regulations to discipline students to study. Employers will discipline the employee to obey or he will be fired. Parents many times will use discipline in anger on their children for obedience. In each one of these cases discipline doesn't show much love. God is love and love has a way of having one under authority wanting to obey.

This is probably the reason Jesus used love in training his disciples. Jesus did admonish them once in a while but never used disciplinary action to force his disciples to be obedient. God's people have been so

disobedient because of a lack of self-discipline. Forced discipline without love causes rebellion. Today we find many disobedient Christians in the church and not many will honor the church if they see godly people as hypocrites. Hypocrisy is one of the main reasons why people do not want to attend church. Seeing hypocrisy in the church takes away their desire from attending church so they stay home and become hypocrites more so than the people in the church.

In my life story, I gave up everything to follow the Lord. Since I couldn't read or understand the Bible I did things that seemed good. Since most Christians looked up to me I continued living my Christian life with good works. I continued that way and it seemed to work because of the many miracles that God had come my way.

There were areas that I had to suffer but that was no different from my past sinful life before I became a Christian. I had no idea that I was disobedient within myself and nobody told me. I was faithful in going to church not knowing anything else was needed. Many of my old habits of lust, materialism, and pride were still present but I kept them a secret.

I needed discipline but no Christian set an example for me. I did start to realize that when others were told they were wrong there was usually reaction. I then realized I was no different. Yet I did hear about self-discipline being very important. My first realization of this was mentioned in my life story. Read Chapter 2 OF MY LIFE STORY subtitled: STARTING A NEW LIFE. God rewarded me for that self-discipline but I couldn't grasp it as being necessary in every area of life.

One day I asked someone how did Jesus discipline Judas. The person said that Jesus did it by loving Judas. That made sense to me but I still had to put the pieces together. Jesus never did tell Judas privately nor did He discipline him. Through love, Jesus wanted Judas to discipline himself. Jesus didn't use disciplinary action like the world does. The love of Jesus is to get us to discipline ourselves because love draws others to mimic Jesus. "If I be lifted up I will draw all men unto me."

Jesus used this method with His disciples then and now also, over 2,000 years later. He is the same yesterday, today and forever. The only difference is His disciples now have Jesus in them and not just with them.

Jesus doesn't force us to do anything. I believe that is why there is so much corruption in the church today. The reason for it is because the church is no better than the world. The way church uses discipline today is the world's way. Every few years most churches in our country have had divisions because of forced discipline. Because of many laws changing, the court favors the sinner over the Christian. This is the reason we need to be in the Word of God daily and to understand that there are daily directions for each one of us. The more we do this the more we can sense Christ's love and the more obedient we will become.

The discipline Jesus wants us to have is in the fruit of the spirit. *Galatians 5:22-23.* Love, joy, peace, patience, gentleness, goodness, faith, meekness and self-control.

You can't have one without the others. This is why self-control is so important. For example, you can't have love without self-discipline. Forced discipline is the world's way, not God's way. If we live in the spirit we will walk in the spirit and have God's love, joy and peace etc. with self-control.

We will never understand God's love without loving our enemies. And there is no way we can love our enemies from the knowledge of the world. I have a couple illustrations of this in my life story. Also see *1 Peter 2:19-25.* We need to do what is right even if we have to suffer for it. Jesus suffered for our sin being without sin.

CHAPTER 95 APOSTASY IN THE USA

When I asked the Lord in what way apostasy affects me, He had much to say. First I had to examine my own life and confess my sins before I saw the whole picture.

Apostasy means complacency, which is satisfying oneself. This accounts for the steady decrease of church attendance since 1957 which was about 70 percent at the time and it is now only 14.5 percent. The attack on September 11, 2001, showed some increase but within a couple of months the spiritual turned back to normal. Apostasy in the church comes from the families that make up the church. If families do not have Christ in the home it will affect the spirit in the church. Most people describe apostasy by how bad things are getting around them and in our government, but knowing what happens during apostasy will not eliminate it. People who talk against our country are seeing the signs of apostasy in our government, in businesses, world conflicts and natural disasters, but we have a hard time examining the church.

We must first see how apostasy is in our own lives and confess it as sin. Can a person sin because of his human nature without temptation? The Bible doesn't seem to answer that question. My worst enemy is within myself. When a person comes to know the Lord, does God forgive him of all his sins? Why does he keep sinning?

Everything is based on the fact God can give us more love, joy and peace than the world can. Does God break all our bad habits or can bad habits be carried over into your Christian life? Many of my old habits have been carried over into my Christian life but why? I never had someone disciple me. The word "disciple" is a noun and so is it in the Gospels. So Jesus couldn't have discipled them because I am using the word disciple as a verb. Discipline is a word similar as disciple and yet the word discipline is not used in the New Testament. The only thing left is that Jesus showed his disciples how to be disciples. Jesus did that by spending much time with his disciples daily.

I have a hard time learning the computer but when someone shows me, it becomes simple. The word discipline is not in the New Testament, but why? We know that discipline is important. But there are two aspects of discipline. One is the world's way and the other is God's way. The world's way is to force discipline on others and God's way is to love us so we would want to apply self-discipline into our lives. That is the fruit of the spirit. The fruit of the spirit is singular that could mean that you can't have one without the others.

Parents go wrong by trying to discipline their children in anger. It doesn't work. Because they will mimic you the wrong way. Sin is passed down by the bad we do and it doesn't matter how good we have been. If parents just make one mistake that is not confessed it will destroy all the good. And children will mimic the bad and this is how sin is passed down. This is why forgiveness should be practiced in the home by first the fathers practicing forgiveness. Telling children they are wrong even in love is not good enough. You must practice what you teach. *Galatians 5:16-21 (KJV)* [16] This I say then, Walk in the Spirit, and ye shall not fulfil the lust of the flesh. [17] For the flesh lusteth against the Spirit, and the Spirit against the flesh: and these are contrary the one to the other: so that ye cannot do the things that ye would. [18] But if ye be led of the Spirit, ye are not under the law. [19] Now the works of the flesh are manifest, which are these; Adultery, fornication, uncleanness, lasciviousness, [20] idolatry, witchcraft, hatred, variance, emulations, wrath, strife, seditions, heresies, [21] envyings, murders, drunkenness, revellings, and such like: of the which I tell you before, as I have also told you in time past, that they which do such things shall not inherit the kingdom of God.

In another translation it says: *Galatians 5:16-18 (GW)* "[16] Let me explain further. Live your life as your spiritual nature directs you. Then you will never follow through on what your corrupt nature wants. [17] What your corrupt nature wants is contrary to what your spiritual nature wants, and what your spiritual nature wants is contrary to what your corrupt nature wants. They are opposed to each other. As a result, you don't always do what you intend to do. [18] If your spiritual nature is your guide, you are not subject to Moses' laws."

THESE ARE SOME OF THE AREAS THE CHURCH IS ENTERING INTO APOSTASY:

[1] Almost every church has had divisions. If we can't love people of different denominations we will not be able to love people of our own church.
[2] There have been no new converts. How did Jesus handle church discipline? It is by love which is very seldom duplicated today.
[3] There is no discipleship if you are not following the way that Jesus did in the Gospels.
[4] There is no forgiveness. The early church practiced forgiveness in each church service.
[5] There is much secret sin in the church.
[6] The love, joy and peace is mostly of the world and not of God.
[7] In America there is not much left of the middle class. What happens to a third world country is that the middle class is wiped out. There are only the rich and the poor.
[8] Families do not include God in daily devotions.
[9] Christians are not using the Scriptures for application.
[10] There is no accountability.
[11] The church uses discipline in a forceful way.
[12] Judging one another is out of hand.
[13] The Fruit of the Spirit is not being applied.

I knew it was wrong to have riches of the world so I gave away all the money I had and I did that five times. I thought that was pretty good but I knew little about the Bible. For the first five years my Christian life was built around my good works. The problem was that I was going to be good in my own strength. For that reason there was no continuous victory. I had to periodically give away all that I had every time I fell into temptation. When lustful thoughts continued I would try in my own efforts to cast them out and I could go for months but I could never have a continuous victory. My main problem was that when I thought I was right I would argue my point. I thought that I had to stand up for what is right. My doctrine was right, like most Christians believe.

Since I was a child I noticed that others were better than me. In grade school I was the only one in the class who couldn't read.

When I tried hard to be better I convinced myself that I was better than others. When I went to the mission field, another missionary told me that I had no business being a missionary because I never was going to learn the language. He was right, but to prove him wrong I did much more than what others would do. I memorized Scripture and witnessed in public much more than the average missionary. That made me think I was better than they were. The sad thing was that it only proved that I didn't love them. When I was first saved, God did a miracle and broke my habits of drinking and smoking immediately. Today I have complete victory over these two things. The sad thing is that in other habits I couldn't maintain a continuous victory. There is something stronger than faith. Without faith it is impossible to please God. But if I had faith to move mountains and have not love it would profit me nothing. And if I gave all my belongings away and sacrificed my own life without love it would profit me nothing.

God's love is not a gift that some people receive and some do not. It doesn't come by works either, but it comes by confessing your sins to God and God is love. *1 John 1:9* If we confess our sins, He is faithful and just to forgive us our sins, and to cleanse us from all unrighteousness.

CHAPTER 96 WHAT MADE CHRISTIANITY ATTRACTIVE IN THE EARLY CHURCH?

I Thessalonians was the first book Paul wrote and we can learn something about what Paul did. Paul didn't get paid when going out as a missionary so he had to find work. The first thing Paul would do when going into town was to look for work. He was a tent maker but probably also worked in small things like making items from leather, such as sandals, wallets and bags.
1 Thessalonians 2:9 "For ye remember, brethren, our labour and travail: for labouring night and day, because we would not be chargeable unto any of you, we preached unto you the gospel of God."

Before the time of Christianity no pagan religion had any emphasis on doctrine. Even the Jewish religion had little emphasis on doctrine, but both the pagan religions and the Jew emphasized application.

The reason why Christianity is based on doctrine was because of the death and resurrection of Jesus Christ. That gave Christians the doctrine of the living God who died and rose from the dead and lived among us. Now Jesus Christ is living in us by the Holy Spirit directing our spirit. The problem is that doctrine has been a continuous process. Doctrine has control over Christians and has put application as a second rate commodity.

In pagan religions there were many gods. Everyone chose his own god but there was no proof that their god was better than someone else's god. The Christians believed in one God that was the God of all the universe and there will be no other gods besides Him. That is why we have the doctrine of the trinity. It was to make the Father, the Son and the Holy Ghost one God.

To this day the Jews believe that Christians have three gods, so we Christians are pagans. The problem with the Jews is that they are disobedient in their application. Their application is based on tradition. They even have a chair for their Messiah at the times of performing their ceremonies.

The reason why the Jews and other religions persecute the Christian is because we put our God above their gods. Jesus never stressed He was God as He witnessed to the pagans. To His followers His stress was on the fact we should love our enemies and not criticize them.

The Christian stress on doctrine has caused much diversity ever since Jesus ascended to heaven. For the first 300 years Christianity was scattered. See *Acts 8:1.* Christianity continued to be scattered until the time of Constantine. During this time the Christians were meeting in small house groups and each group had their own doctrine.

When Constantine became emperor and legalized Christianity he wanted everyone to have the same Bible so he had wise men search the manuscripts and canonized one New Testament, forming 27 books which we have today. The problem is that it didn't help unify Christians. We are still hearing of doctrinal emphasis which only divides the church. The church is either making new doctrines or finding the denomination they like the best which has them despise other denominations.

What made Christianity spread was not their doctrine but the power of God showing miracles. When Christ had his ministry most of the miracles were in public.

Today miracles are not the convicting factor of the power of God any longer. Rarely does God allow miracles in the church today. The major prayer request is healing but instant healing seldom occurs. Could it be the reason is that the church isn't taking the Gospel publicly any longer?

When the Roman Empire made Christianity legal about 50 percent of the world became Christians within a few generations. This is when a separation started between clergy and laity. Clergy preached and laity listened.

The preaching was only by educated men because the Bible was so difficult to understand and had to be taught by educated men. That was the reason the Bible was not put into the hands of laity and continued that way until the time of Martin Luther. The

Catholic Church continued this practice until the late 1940s.

Today every Christian has a Bible in their home, yet most people tell me that they do not understand the Scriptures. At least this is what they tell me in my daily witnessing.

Doctrine is important but first it must be backed up by Jesus, the founder of Christianity. The whole Bible is inspired but that doesn't mean that the Biblical writers of the Bible were perfect in being like Jesus. The stress on Doctrine is what Jesus said in the Gospels of Matthew, Mark, Luke, and John, that the main commandment or doctrine is to love God, and the second is for men to love one another. In Corinthians 13 Paul put love above all and then hope and then faith.

Today the church has little love for all men. We should love our enemies and today our greatest enemies are disobedient Christians living in sin. Instead of the church dealing with sin the right way there have been many divisions because of conflict over doctrine, preference and tradition.

Before Christianity, no pagan religion had any emphasis on doctrine. Even the Jewish religion had no emphasis on doctrine. The Jews stressed worship and daily practice. The reason why Christianity practiced doctrine was because of the death and resurrection of Jesus Christ. Confirmation is the proof of the death and resurrection of Jesus. It was mentioned many times in the Old Testament and in the New Testament. Jesus told his disciples several times that it was expedient for Him to die. In the pagan religions there were many gods and every one had their own god, or gods. But what happened was that Christians believed in only one God so they believed that they were the only right religion. This is where persecution comes in regarding other religions and dictators who wanted everybody to worship the king or queen. Jesus offset that by saying that we need to love our enemies. Condemning other religions was not Christ's teaching. In the Old Testament both the Jewish people and the pagan religions set aside doctrine to stress practical application and not on right doctrine.

The early church in the first three centuries had so much diversity in doctrine because they knew the death and resurrection of Jesus was the basis of our salvation and growth. But seemingly doctrine didn't matter much because the whole Roman Empire was evangelized.

When Constantine became emperor he thought Christian doctrine had to be centralized. To do this they had the doctrine of the Trinity and they canonized the New Testament. But that didn't help because different doctrine made Christians look down on one another as heretics.

Paul told the people that idols were not gods. Religion with the pagans was what god could do for them on this earth. The afterlife was not a reality and there was no doctrine to have emphasis on afterlife. In the New Testament Christians have hope of eternal life. In Titus 1:2 eternal life had become a main doctrine in Christianity. Pagan religions put all their stress on what god could do for them on this earth.

What attracted people to Doctrine was the many miracles. Just one miracle healing would stir up the whole city. After the mass conversions at the day of Pentecost, the Christians had persecution and they spread out and converts were mostly individuals. Christians had different doctrines but there was obedience to God's Word. In the first 300 years all the Roman Empire was evangelized and 5 to 7 percent of the about 80 million population became Christians.

When the Roman Empire made Christianity legal, about 50 percent of the empire became Christian in the next few generations.

CHAPTER 97 CAN CHRISTIANS FORGIVE THE SINS OF OTHERS?

John 20.23 "Whosesoever sins you forgive they are forgiven them and whosesoever sins you retain they are retained."

This doesn't mean we humans can forgive the sins of others. But it does mean if we forgive others of their offensive sins toward us, it will draw them to Christ. Also Christ will forgive our sins. *Matthew 5:14-15* "For if you forgive men their trespasses, your heavenly Father will also forgive you. [15] but if you forgive not men their trespasses, neither will your Father forgive your trespasses."

CHAPTER 98 LOVE IS THE GREATEST BUT WHAT IS THE SECOND GREATEST?

In *first Corinthians 13:13* it says "Faith, hope and love. These three but the greatest is love." If it is in that order then "hope" is the second greatest commandment. Remember hope is expectation or to expect something from God. Faith is for now. When somebody knows he is wrong he must stop doing that activity. Hope is for the future. This is why daily devotions are so necessary. God assigns us problems to be resolved. When we go to Him in prayer and the Bible we tell Jesus of our problems and He will show us the solution. The Bible will give us directions for the future. For this reason families need the Bible daily.

Hebrew words for (hope) in the Old Testament mean anything from trust to expectation. In the New Testament it means only expect or expectation. To expect something means the future, and especially short-term future. For example: If the family can't seem to resolve their problems, the father then tells the family that they will read a chapter from the Bible and see how the Scriptures are directing them by what the Holy Spirit is saying to show them how to resolve the problem.

They can tell the children they can use their imagination and even have the small children draw something on paper. This will not be doctrine but an application for the problem, then talk about it until the whole family is in agreement. This may take some time in prayer and meditation but they will have expectation that the Holy Spirit will bring the family into oneness. In *John 17* there are 26 verses which talk about the Father, the Son and the Holy Spirit working in us to be one. In the 26 verses it talks about these three persons over 167 times and the emphasis is to be in unity as one. The strange thing is the Holy Spirit is not mentioned once in this chapter but when it talks about the believer, it is the Holy Spirit working in us to make us one with the Son and the Father. The three characters in John 17 are the Father, the Son and the believer.

Salvation is not confessing our sins but Jesus forgiving us of our sins that put Christ on the cross. All He wants from us is a thank you. As we start living for the Lord, our asking for forgiveness will be a continuous thing until we die. Each time we confess our sin we become righteous because we are forgiven from all unrighteousness according to *1 John 1:9*.

How could we nail Jesus on the cross over 2,000 years ago? We don't understand this but it shows the greatness of God. To Him time means nothing. He is the same yesterday, today and forever. Jesus also died for the people who haven't been born as yet.

CHAPTER 99 LOVE STIRS UP

Most couples date to get to know the person they want to marry. Three times in the Book of Solomon it says: "Don't awaken love before the time."

Is love mental, psychological, spiritual, or is it totally emotional? Why is it that you are attracted to some people and not others? Sometimes it is beauty, personality, intelligence or the person likes the same things that you do. There is a difference between friendship and romantic love.

The three references from the book of Solomon are: *Solomon 2:7, 3:3 & 8:4* and the following statement is repeated each time: "Stir not up nor awake my love until he

pleases." One translation says this: "Dear women of Jerusalem promise me by the power by the deer and gazelles never to awaken love before it is ready."

There are three main characters in the Book of Solomon: there is the Shulammite woman, there is King Solomon, who is called the shepherd, and there are the daughters of Jerusalem who are trying to pull the Shulammite woman from the shepherd who she loves.

It is Solomon who dresses up like a shepherd. Solomon calls her my sister and my spouse. Spouse in the Bible means someone who you were engaged to. In Jewish culture the moment you were engaged, you were married. There was a time for testing where the man and the woman could not see each other.

This time was nine months to a year. This was to prove faithfulness. And if she was unfaithful you had to give her a divorcement. After that time the father went to fetch the bridegroom and brought him to the bride. This is why when Mary was pregnant with the Holy Spirit, Joseph was about to divorce her but the Lord told him that it was alright to marry her.

Do not have romantic love before the time. Romantic love is reserved for the person you are going to marry. What we have not been taught is the danger of being romantic before that time. It can have you marry before you know the person. Didn't your father try to warn you when it was before the time? When you allow emotion to come your decisions will be based on feelings.

Feelings before facts is bad, the right order is: Faith, fact and then feelings. It is so easy to put the cart before the horse. Faith is by God's Word, which is fact, and then the feelings. Satan always wants the feeling to come first.

Many couples do not know much about each other and that takes time. The spirit is willing to teach us but the flesh is weak. Feeling without God's direction will get us in trouble. In dating it is easy to give your heart to someone, but it is not your whole heart. Your hobbies, sports and other interests are still part of your love which your spouse has no interest in. So after romance leaves so does the oneness leave. Men and woman think differently. Women are good for things around the house. Men like mechanics and do not like housework, but they both have to be done. One needs to praise the other for these things.

Kids fall in love with classroom sweethearts at the time one has feeling for the opposite sex. The number of high school pregnancies are countless. Many live with broken hearts, depression and anxiety.

Marriage is a blood covenant. Blood covenant means one time which is forever. Jesus shed His blood once for all mankind. Read *Romans 6:9-10*.

Dating is where two are alone together and emotions are not under control. Courting is not being alone until marriage. This helps control emotions. This is for accountability which is needed to eliminate secret sin and for emotions not to get carried away. Because our culture allows dating, here is what happens: 13-year-old girls who have lost their virginity and are easy targets in public schools for guys who have one thing on their minds.

Boys are hunters by nature. They hunt for deer and will hunt until they get one. When he gets it he cuts the head off and puts it in his living room for a trophy. Then he invites people over so he can brag how he conquered that deer. The same in dating, the girl becomes the deer, or in this case d-e-a-r. Once the fellow conquerors her he will brag about it. Then he finds another and another.

You are not a man to lust but one to love others the way Jesus loved us. You can't have God's love without temperance. Temperance is self-control. The Fruit of the Spirit starts with love and ends with self-control. God's love does not come without our self-control. We cast down what is of Satan and replace it with God's Word. See *2 Corinthians 10:5*.

In dating there are so many broken hearts which put life on hold and that can last a long time. Rejection comes in, then depression, and then anxiety. In public schools boys and girls mix together with little supervision during lunch or on the school grounds. Every parent must have discipleship with their children by teaching them temperance or self-control. Not just teaching it but mainly by showing it in their own lives. Jesus did this by being with His disciples daily. The best teaching for children is right in their own home, by teaching God's Word and the parents being an example. It takes time to show discipleship. The church puts little emphasis on this.

Fellows are attracted to girls mostly by feelings and lust. There are dangers in not disciplining yourself concerning lust. When one finally finds a soul mate, he or she will compare them to others that they dated in the past. Also you can carry over sinful practices in your marriage that you can't get out of your mind. These images can be brought up any time you want them.

We all have the freedom of choice. One of our choices is who we listen to. There are voices that we must choose from: There are voices of people around us, the voice of God and the voice of Satan. The voice around us is peer pressure. The voice of God brings direction and discernment. Then the voice of Satan which is the voice of rebellion. In *1 Thess. 5:22* the whole person is made up of the body, soul and the spirit. The correct voice comes from God's spirit talking to our spirit. "God is a Spirit and they that worship Him must worship Him is Spirit and Truth."

But Satan is a spirit also and we must know who is speaking to us. Satan's voice will appeal to the flesh. God's Spirit talks but we need spiritual ears to listen. *Rev. 2-3* "He that has an ear let him hear what the spirit says." Each of the seven churches in Revelation states this as the final conclusion.

Young people do not know any other way than dating. There was a day when no one knew what dating was. Why, because courting was the only way. After a while courting was old-fashioned and today people know nothing else. In courting there is little or no physical contact. Dating is hinged on physical contact. Dating became strong in the 1950s. This is when people started to say that courting was old-fashioned. Courting is getting to know the other person intellectually, spiritually and to know everything about the person.

Dating is mainly the attraction for each other and when the flesh is stimulated there is no room for anything else. If Jesus had some ladies as disciples the men would listen to Jesus but not hear a word He was saying. This is the only way to learn self-control, you can love each other without touching. If you try to love by both touch and companionship, touch will win out. You learn to love your enemy the same way. Not by your emotions but by the truth. The truth is to love your enemies.

Dating in America became popular during the time of drive-in movies. Teens could legally park in public with no restrictions concerning romance.

Many young couples think they can live on love. Being together is all that matters. Responsibilities in marriage are not recognized until it is too late. They think they can live on love. They say, "We love each other so much we know everything will work out." The problem is when the romance wears off and the problems come they are unprepared and then come the disagreements and arguments. Their love is superficial. It is like a child's love. A child likes to receive and still wants more. Your love still wants more but is not satisfied. Now, it is hard to see the love you once had for each other. In *1 Corinthians 7* it says when I was a child I understood as a child, I spoke as a child, I thought as a child but when I became a man I put away childish things. Now they are vulnerable to someone wanting to take advantage of them.

Love is heavily connected to feelings and emotions which go directly to the brain. It is the brain that makes us feel that we are in love. And the feelings are so strong that no one can tell you that your love relationship is wrong. Not even God. Love is one of the strongest drives in human nature but it comes way short for what God wants for a marriage.

The brain has a part called the caudate nucleus. It has receptors for a neutron transmitter which is called dopamine. Dopamine is where we get the word "drugs" from. When people get hooked on drugs the brain releases dopamine. Dopamine is a chemical from the caudate nucleus and spreads this chemical throughout the brain. This gives a person feelings of acceleration, a feeling of energy, of focus and will affect the reward part of the brain. So if dopamine is released it makes you feel great. The dopamine is through out the mind so you can't think any other way. The subconscious mind can't bring back memories of the past, so you can't logically think with understanding.

You have a deep desire to get marriage even on your first date. But in reality there was no intimate conversation or spiritual connection with each other.

This is what the dopamine can do to your mind but the chemical will eventual stop flowing when separated for a while. The only way you can feel good again is to be around that person physically. But the more you are with the person you need to go a step further in love-making to have the same feeling as before. Now you want sexual involvement having no control of yourself. This is where the romances wears off and the genuine love starts but not without self-discipline. The fruit of the spirit starts with love and ends with self-control. One can't have God's genuine love just with romance.

Pornography has the same chemical going into action. But to stay at the same level of satisfaction one must see other pictures. This is always the case. One gets deeper into it but is never satisfied. Pornography is a drug because it acts the same way as drugs. This is true with any sin.

Sin of any kind doesn't stay at the same level. Sin becomes more and more sinful. This is the way Satan wants to destroy us by having us destroy ourselves. We can see deception in others much easier than we can see it in ourselves.

It is actually under God's control. God doesn't allow Satan to tempt two Christians the same way at the same time. In this way if Christians are working together they will be able to see what Satan is planning but there must be harmony between Christians.

Our human nature is to judge one another when we see our Christian brother in sin. The result is a reaction rather than harmony. But Satan knows this so he finds a way he can kill two birds with the same stone by having two Christians that can work together be tempted differently to create disunity. In this the Lord is telling us that we need one another.

This is the way Satan is destroying the church. The sin of one Christian causing sin in another Christian. This is explained in previous chapters.

This is why after marriage when each tries every possible way to obtain enjoyment for him or herself, there is nothing left to keep the marriage together. Many will go outside the marriage for love fulfillment or build a deeper interest for sports or a hobby. Of course the Holy Spirit is still drawing the person to Himself. The problem is the person wants to keep his motivation for love through lust. Human nature want self-satisfaction, not self-discipline.

The Holy Spirit leads us into self-control. The choice we have is love for this world or love for God. See *1 John 2:15-16*. The love for anything in this world is first stimulated by feelings. Love for God comes by an unseen spiritual power called faith.

John 17 tells us over and over again that Jesus wants us to be one with Him as He is one with the Father. But also that we should be one with one another. The difference is that earthly marriage is restricted to bring only two people together in love.

Godly marriage is to bring all His creation together in oneness that can't be expressed with the word "love." This is why in the Greek, God's love is all together a different word. In English we have to figure it out for ourselves. All the love that is in this world is connected to lust. Lust is love for ourselves. We can't understand that. *Ephesians 3:19* "And to know the love of Christ which passes knowledge that we might be filled with all the fullness of God."

When I told one fellow that there will be no marriages in heaven, he quickly responded, "Then I don't want to go to heaven." He knew no other love.

There are feelings for God's love but it comes by faith first. That means we must have control over lust. If we do not discipline our thinking we will never come into the feeling for God's love. We need to think how great God's love is and remember it is the opposite of lust. *2 Corinthians 10:5* in the Bible says to cast down Lust and bring every thought to the obedience to God's love. That is a paraphrase. When we build up our faith God will give us a love to obey His commandments. Today men put too much confidence in the doctrine of men. Jesus said several times be careful of the doctrine of men. Doctrine of men has started many cults. It has also put much disagreement between the many different fundamental denominations.

God's love doesn't stay at the same level either. As we grow in the love of God we desire less of the love of the world. Love and obedience cannot be separated. Because of God's love heaven is full of praise. The Pharisees didn't think so when they told Jesus to stop his disciples from being disorderly. Jesus said that if He stopped them the stones would cry out. God's love when manifested will be a way of living in satisfaction more than this world can begin to offer.

To have an understanding of God's love we need to become familiar with the nine Beatitudes of Matthew 5:1-13. They are progressions. You can't have one without the preceding ones. And the last one, which is really the last two Beatitudes, is the top character quality of Christ. That is to love people who come against you. The first qualification to love your enemy is to confess your sin of not being able to. To try to love your enemy is your own strength will make it seem more impossible. Jesus said, what is impossible with man is possible with God.

The lust of this world will affect our logical reasoning. Rejecting God's love eventually will have you think irrationally. Wrong becomes right and right becomes wrong. This is called a reprobate mind. A man will steal a car and then flee the police doing 100 mph thinking that he can escape.

This can make a person enter into the unpardonable sin. Rich people that use their money for lust think of suicide because they use their money to satisfy themselves and they are starved for real love. They have rejected the only love that can help them. This is what happened to Judas. Jesus said that it would better that Judas was never born. That was the only way to escape the Lake of fire. We cannot turn back time so Judas had to take his own life. He didn't have any love to keep himself alive. It would have been different if Judas confessed his sin to Jesus instead of the chief priest.

The transformation between human love and God's love is found in the nine Beatitudes. The Beatitudes are progressions. One needs the proceeding ones to go to the next level. The highest level is to love your persecutor.

In the same way the fruit of the Spirit is nine. This number is mentioned in the singular tense. You can't have love without self-discipline or the other seven.

In heaven we will never be bored or depressed but God's love will not be a continuous flow in this world. God's love will periodically give us a joy unspeakable but it will not be continuously with us on this earth. Satan's way of defeating us is by trying to prevent these intervals of God's presence. If Satan can take control of the mind continuously our existence will go from bad to worse.

The best way to be relieved from Satan's control is to praise God. There are about 2,000 verses on praise in the Bible. I have about 600 of them on a recording. When I listen to them I become part of the Scripture as I repeat them in thought. God just loves to hear the praises of His people.

One morning when I woke up I felt very depressed. We humans tend to live in the' 'now' of time. The blessing God gave me the day before seemed to be gone and depression had a grip on me. I had to discipline myself to have devotions that morning.

As I continued in the final stages of editing my book I became dizzy. I had to stop editing and as I sat there doing nothing it got worse until I dropped to the floor. I became helpless as my mind kept spinning. I wanted to call someone but I was helpless to do so. I must have laid there for 15 minutes. I slowly was able to get back into my chair and after sitting there for a while I made it to my bed where I spent the rest of the day. The next day I went to the hospital where they examined me for hours. When they saw I couldn't take it any longer I was permitted to lay down.

I was told that I had a disease called vertigo. There was no cure for it but they told me that the body usually heals itself. I spent a couple more days in bed but now well enough to pray about my condition with an open Bible. I discovered that a person doesn't have to fall into depression but with the constant temptation weakness and depression sets in.

I read Chapter four of Matthew concerning the temptations of Jesus: After Jesus was tempted, here is what happened:
Matthew 4:11 The devil left Jesus and the angels came to ministered to Him. Matthew 4:13-14 Jesus entered into the land of the Gentiles and said that the people that lived in darkness had light come upon them.

Matthew 4:17 Jesus preached: "repent for the Kingdom of Heaven is at hand." Matthew 4:19 Jesus said: "follow me and I will make you fishers of men." Matthew 4:23-24 Jesus healed all the sick and those possessed of devils. In Matthew 4:11 Jesus became weak because of the temptation. In Matthew 4:13-14 Jesus predicts that He would transfer the commission to the Gentiles. In Matthew 4:17 Jesus started his public ministry preaching repentance. In Matthew 4:19 Jesus selected His disciples to make them fishers of men. Jesus was only called to the Jewish people. See Matthew 15:24, but above in Matthew 14:13-14 Jesus had transferred the commission from the Jew to the Gentile. Yet all through the Gospels Jesus was giving His chosen people a last opportunity but through their disobedience the commission was transferred to the Gentile by the Apostle Paul.

Today after over 2,000 years the Gentiles are given a warning of their disobedience but they will reject it and the commission will be transferred back to the Jewish people. No doubt some Gentile will go to their reward. But the Bible says few there will be that enter into eternal life. Broad is the way that enter into destruction and many will enter into eternal damnation.

When Jesus came to earth He lived among His chosen people giving them of a last chance to come out of their disobedience. At first most of the Jewish people believe in Jesus as their Messiah but when Jesus had more followers then the Jewish leaders had they were jealous. Jealousy led to anger which brought them to the decision to kill him.

Jesus was only called to the lost sheep of Israel but because of their rebellion the commission to spread the Truth to the world was transferred to the Gentiles.

The Great Commission was given to the Gentiles to go into all the world but the United States after 2,000 years have entered into complacency which is called the apostate church.

Now God is warning us Gentiles as he did His own chosen people. It is sad that the church hasn't received that warning. The church knows we are living in the apostate age. Most churches I have attended say they are doing the best they can.

The church knows the end is near. Most churches understand according to Scriptures that the commission is going to be handed back to the Jewish nation because of the Gentiles disobedience of not making Christ known as Jesus had showed in the Scriptures This will happen just before the second coming of Christ.

The church should hasten the second coming of Christ but the Gentile couldn't see their own rebellion. 2 Peter 3:12 "Looking for and hasting into the coming of the day of God, wherein the heavens being on fire shall be dissolved, and elements shall melt with fervent heat?" Hasting means to speed up the second coming of Christ.

How many Christians of this generation will go to heaven I do not know? But the Bible says broad is the way that enter into destruction and few will find eternal life. See Matthew 7:14 and 7:21-23

Shortly after my experience with vertigo I have had a visitation of the Holy Spirit. I never had been so happy. I can understand what Paul said: It would be far better to be with the Lord but it is needful to live in this world a while longer to make known Christ's ways.

35858225R10060

Made in the USA
San Bernardino, CA
07 July 2016